Trn

Series Three: Cultural Memory

Volume 1

The White Rose
Reading, Writing, Resistance

Edited by Alexandra Lloyd

Series editor: Henrike Lähnemann

Published in June 2019 by Taylor Institution Library.

Copyright © Taylor Institution Library 2019

http://www.bodleian.ox.ac.uk/taylor

www.whiteroseproject.org

ISBN 978-0-9954564-4-0

Taylor Institution Library, St Giles, Oxford, OX1 3NA

CONTENTS

Acknowledgements

There are several people and organisations without whom this book would not have been possible. Thanks are due to the Taylor Institution Library, the Bodleian Library (particularly colleagues in the Bibliographical Press and the exhibitions team), Hinksey Catholic Parish, the Faculty of Medieval and Modern Languages, the Oxford German Network, St Edmund Hall, the Bundesarchiv, and the Weiße Rose Stiftung, all of whom supported the project in various ways. I am extremely grateful to the contributors, and to colleagues within and beyond Oxford, especially Rey Conquer, Henrike Lähnemann, and Nicola Thomas. Emma Huber's contribution is immeasurable: from her initial enthusiasm and encouragement when I first suggested this project, to her careful preparation of the volume and work behind the scenes.

Above all I wish to thank the student translators for their dedication and commitment. It was a joy and a privilege to work with them on this material. I hope that our volume will contribute to keeping alive the memory of the White Rose and spreading its story beyond Germany. *Es lebe die Freiheit!*

Alexandra Lloyd
Oxford, 9 May 2019

FOREWORD
Hildegard Kronawitter

'Give my last regards to all my friends. They should continue what we have begun.' This was the request Willi Graf made to his sister Anneliese on 12 October 1943, the day of his execution. Decades later, in 1987, Anneliese Knoop-Graf established the Weiße Rose Stiftung (White Rose Foundation) in Munich, together with other relatives and friends, and individuals who had been convicted of involvement in the resistance. Those of us who today are responsible for this work are bound by our charter to fulfil Willi Graf's intention through our commemorative activities. We aim to make known the White Rose's resistance to the National Socialist dictatorship in Germany and abroad, and to promote tolerance, civil courage and personal responsibility in state and society. More broadly, our endeavour is to spread the resistance group's timeless message of freedom in the present day. I am therefore grateful to Dr Alexandra Lloyd of Magdalen College and St Edmund Hall, University of Oxford, for her dedication under the banner of the White Rose, especially her work with students.

The White Rose was a circle of friends centred around the students Hans Scholl and Alexander Schmorell at the Ludwig Maximilian University in Munich. These young people met each other in 1942 as students. They were from middle-class backgrounds and had a Christian humanist outlook; they were interested in literature and music, and were neither members of any particular political organisation nor can they be ascribed to one. In the summer of 1942 and again in January and February 1943, they wrote, made copies of, and distributed pamphlets opposing the National Socialist dictatorship and called for an end to the war. Willi Graf, Sophie Scholl and Alexander Schmorell took the pamphlets to other cities where amongst their wider circle of friends they found those who would in turn help them by copying and further distributing the texts. Professor Kurt Huber, a musicologist and philosopher at the Ludwig Maximilian University joined the resistance group at the end of 1942 and wrote the sixth pamphlet. In the summer of 1943, millions of copies of this text were dropped by the RAF over Germany. Over the course of two nights in February 1943, Hans Scholl, Alexander Schmorell, and Willi Graf used green and black coal-tar dyes to write graffiti on the walls of several Munich buildings. Slogans such as 'Down with Hitler!', 'Freedom!', and 'Hitler Mass-murderer!' were intended to awaken the German people's spirit of resistance, which ultimately proved to be as fruitless as the distribution of the pamphlets. When on 18 February 1943 Hans and Sophie deposited pamphlets around the atrium of the main Munich university building, they were arrested by the Gestapo. Subsequently the whole resistance group was broken up.

The courageous and clear-sighted protest by these young people and their professor was severely punished by the National Socialist judiciary acting as the henchman of the dictatorship: in multiple trials, seven individuals from the resistance group were sentenced to death by the People's Court and guillotined. Over twenty others who had been involved were convicted, some receiving long prison sentences. Further to the Munich prosecutions, another 30 people were arrested in Hamburg in autumn 1943, and imprisoned for several months. In a final trial at the People's Court, on 17 April 1945 a further death sentence was pronounced. The condemned man, Heinz Kucharski, was however able to escape in time. All those White Rose members who remained in prison were finally freed by the Allies at the end of April 1945.

The first four pamphlets bore the title 'Pamphlets of the White Rose'. As Hans Scholl said in his Gestapo interrogation, the name was chosen because it 'sounded good', while also suggesting that 'there was a programme behind it'. From 1952 Inge Aicher-Scholl, Hans and Sophie's sister, cemented the resistance group's name permanently with her publication *Weiße Rose*. Previously they had been spoken of as the 'student resistance' or the 'Scholl Affair'.

As early as autumn 1945 the first newspaper articles appeared in Germany about the group's resistance, and on 4 November 1945, a large-scale memorial service was held at the instigation of family members. Soon, the squares outside the university were renamed by the City of Munich after the Scholl siblings and Professor Kurt Huber. A year later the university honoured the seven who had been executed with a commemorative plaque. In the decades that followed, schools, streets and cultural institutions were named after the main figures of the White Rose, above all the Scholl siblings.

Over the years, individuals who had been condemned as part of the resistance, such as Marie-Luise Jahn, Franz J. Müller, and Hans Hirzel, and relatives such as Anneliese Knoop-Graf and Inge Aicher-Scholl spoke as witnesses, garnering great empathy for those who had been executed, especially among young people. From 1968 historians took up the subject of the resistance group. Christian Petry published *Studenten aufs Schafott: Die Weiße Rose und ihr Scheitern* (*Students on the Scaffold: The Defeat of the White Rose*) and provoked a media scandal, because of his analysis of the reasons why this resistance had had no effect. Since then countless monographs and biographies have been published. New publications on the White Rose still find readers in Germany. Alexandra Lloyd's book gives me reason to hope that interest in the White Rose will grow in Great Britain too.

Films, too, have drawn younger generations to the resistance group. Michael Verhoeven's *Die Weiße Rose* (*The White Rose*, 1981) and Marc Rothemund's *Sophie Scholl — Die letzten Tage* (*Sophie Scholl — The Final Days*, 2005) have garnered international attention. In Munich there is a prestigious annual book prize, the Geschwister-Scholl Preis (Scholl Sibling Prize) which is awarded to a book 'which promotes civic freedom, moral, intellectual, and aesthetic courage, and fosters a responsible awareness of present-day issues' ('das geeignet ist bürgerliche Freiheit, moralischen, intellektuellen und ästhetischen Mut zu fördern und dem verantwortungsvollen Gegenwartsbewusstsein wichtige Impulse zu geben'). These criteria describe precisely how the message of the White Rose is understood today and why the pamphlets, with their reference to freedom, responsibility, justice, and humanity, remain important.

Since 1997, the DenkStätte Weiße Rose (White Rose memorial exhibition) has been located next to the atrium of the Ludwig Maximilian University, where on 18 February Hans and Sophie Scholl distributed the sixth pamphlet and were consequently arrested. The White Rose Foundation maintains the permanent exhibition, which tells the story of the group through documents, images, texts, and interactive media installations. It makes visible the context of the Nazi dictatorship and its war crimes, as well as the history of those ideas which influenced the group. It presents the biographies of the key individuals, and shows the network of resistance which reached other cities beyond Munich. In 2018, the DenkStätte had over 47,000 visitors, a third of whom came from abroad.

For over twenty years, our travelling exhibition 'The White Rose: Students against Hitler 1942/43' has been a central means of disseminating the history of the White Rose and their message to the world. Forty-seven display boards in seven languages are available to external partners for displays in schools, colleges, exhibition spaces and other educational institutions. Currently the travelling exhibition is in Spain, Italy, the US, and Russia. We work with teachers and pupils on pedagogical projects in schools as part of an experience-led 'learning from history' programme. Young people contextualise and enhance their knowledge of the Third Reich through their own historical research and archival work. The commitment of teachers is essential to the success of the project.

As with other educational institutions, the White Rose Foundation uses social media. Our homepage, www.weisse-rose-stiftung.de, had around 460,000 visitors in 2018 and on Facebook our weekly posts reach our 4300 'friends'. In 2018, the 75th anniversary of the White Rose, there were extensive media reports about the resistance group, and it goes without saying that we are always delighted to engage with the media.

Our events bring to the fore many important themes from the context of the White Rose. We present newly published monographs or biographies about the group, and together with the university, we organise the annual memorial organ concert with readings on the 22 February. We commemorate the anniversaries of death of the most important participants, and their centenaries. From time to time we work with theatre groups as most recently with the Munich Volkstheater's production, *Sophie Scholl: Love in the Time of Resistance.*

Why does the White Rose, much more so than other German resistance groups, receive so much attention, making it possible for those who have come after to identify with it? The historian Wolfgang Benz takes a critical view of this, suggesting that after the end of the Nazi regime, the resistance circle were used as 'representatives for a kind of attitude deemed appropriate for moral aspiration, as a goal for political education, and as a humanist imperative'.[1] Beyond this socio-political assessment, at the White Rose Foundation we see how through our work the dreadful fate of the students and Professor Huber affects young people in particular. It helps them to understand how the loss of freedom for an individual is bound up with dictatorship, circumscribed freedom of opinion, intolerance, and lack of empathy for others. They rightly conclude that racism, xenophobia, and the deceptive simplicity of extreme right-wing politics can only be countered when individuals behave humanely.

Dr Hildegard Kronawitter
Vorsitzende Weiße Rose Stiftung, Munich
(Chair, White Rose Foundation)

---

[1] 'Er wurde stellvertretend in Anspruch genommen für eine Haltung, die als moralischer Anspruch, als Ziel politischer Bildung, als humanistischer Imperativ gültig wurde', Wolfgang Benz, *Im Widerstand: Größe und Scheitern der Opposition gegen Hitler* (Munich: Beck, 2014), p. 353.

INTRODUCTION

Alexandra Lloyd

The White Rose resistance stretched far beyond Munich, but at its heart were six individuals: students Hans Scholl (1918–1943), and Sophie Scholl (1921–1943), who were brother and sister, Christoph Probst (1919–1943), Alexander Schmorell (1917–1943), and Willi Graf (1918–1943), and Professor Kurt Huber (1893–1943).

Between 1942 and 1943 the group wrote and disseminated six pamphlets calling on the German people to resist Nazism.[1] They used a second-hand duplicating machine, and despite wartime shortages obtained paper, envelopes, stencils, and stamps. They distributed the pamphlets at great personal risk. On 18 February 1943 Hans Scholl and Sophie Scholl took copies of the sixth pamphlet to the University of Munich and deposited them around the atrium at the entrance of the main university building. They were spotted by a university caretaker and detained. Their arrest followed, and on 22 February Hans and Sophie Scholl and Christoph Probst were sentenced to death and executed by guillotine just hours after the conclusion of their trial. Alexander Schmorell, Kurt Huber, and Willi Graf were subsequently arrested, tried, and sentenced to death on 19 April. Schmorell and Huber were executed three months later, on 13 July, and Graf was kept alive in solitary confinement and executed on 12 October 1943.

---

[1] The German term is 'Flugblätter' which can be translated as 'pamphlet' or 'leaflet'. Both words are used interchangeably in this volume.

The pamphlets reflect the development of the group's approach and the changing situation as the war progressed. They draw on a range of philosophical ideas and influences, and include quotations from German writers such as Goethe, Schiller, and Novalis, as well as Aristotle, the Old Testament, and the ancient Chinese philosopher Laozi. The first four pamphlets were written by Hans Scholl and Alexander Schmorell between June and July 1942. Each begins with the heading 'Pamphlets of the White Rose' ('Flugblätter der Weißen Rose') and a corresponding number, suggesting that, from the very beginning, they had intended to produce a *series* of pamphlets. All but the final pamphlet, written by Kurt Huber, end with instructions to the reader to make and distribute further copies of it: from 'We urge you to transcribe this pamphlet, make as many copies as you can and distribute them' to 'Support the resistance movement, <u>distribute</u> the pamphlets.'[2]

The pamphlets were designed to stir up the people, to confront them with truths which the group believed they were deliberately ignoring, through fear or obstinacy. From the very beginning, their language is forceful, even shocking: 'If every one of us waits for someone else to start, then the heralds of avenging Nemesis will draw ever closer until the last sacrificial victim is vainly

---

[2] 'Wir bitten Sie, dieses Blatt mit möglichst vielen Durchschlägen abzuschreiben und weiterzuverteilen!'; 'Unterstützt die Widerstandsbewegung, <u>verbreitet</u> die Flugblätter!' (emphasis original). German quotations are taken from the original pamphlets which are reprinted in this volume. The English translations used here are those undertaken by the White Rose Project student translators, also included in full below.

thrown into the jaws of a demon that will never be sated'.[3] In the second pamphlet, they explicitly denounce the persecution of European Jews, writing: 'since the conquest of Poland, three hundred thousand Jews have been murdered in that country in the most bestial manner. Here, we see the most horrific crime against human dignity, a crime unparalleled in all of human history.'[4] They attempt to show how their fellow Germans have been taken in by Nazism, and urge readers to open their eyes to the atrocities being committed in the name of the regime:

> Until the outbreak of the war, the vast majority of the German people were blinded, the National Socialists did not show their true face, but now, since they have been seen for what they are, the highest and only duty, the most sacred duty even, of every German, must be to destroy these beasts.[5]

Elsewhere, they openly mock the Nazis, poking fun at Adolf Hitler's *Mein Kampf*. It is 'a book which, despite having been written in the most appalling German that I have ever read, has been elevated to

---

[3] 'Wenn jeder wartet, bis der andere anfängt, werden die Boten der rächenden Nemesis unaufhaltsam näher und näher rücken, dann wird auch das letzte Opfer sinnlos in den Rachen des unersättlichen Dämons geworfen sein'.

[4] '[S]eit der Eroberung Polens [sind] dreihunderttausend Juden in diesem Land auf bestialischste Art ermordet worden. Hier sehen wir das fürchterlichste Verbrechen an der Würde des Menschen, ein Verbrechen, dem sich kein ähnliches in der ganzen Menschengeschichte an die Seite stellen kann' (emphasis original).

[5] 'Bis zum Ausbruch des Krieges war der größte Teil des deutschen Volkes geblendet, die Nationalsozialisten zeigten sich nicht in ihrer wahren Gestalt, doch jetzt, da man sie erkannt hat, muss es die einzige und höchste Pflicht, ja heiligste Pflicht eines jeden Deutschen sein, diese Bestien zu vertilgen'.

biblical status by this nation of poets and philosophers'.[6] 'Land der Dichter und Denker' ('nation of poets and philosophers') is an almost proverbial phrase applied to the Germans by themselves. That they have thus embraced this worthless book suggests either that they are not so gifted, or that they need to recover their critical faculties. The pamphlets call on readers to engage in passive resistance, to bring down National Socialism and to bring an end to the war. They advocate sabotage, of factories, NS events, universities, cultural events, the arts, and the media. They even warn against giving to charity street collections, because this will only continue to benefit and support the state.

Several individuals influenced the group, among them Theodor Haecker, an authority on Kierkegaard and translator of John Henry Cardinal Newman. Under the Nazis, Haecker was banned from speaking publicly or publishing. He kept a secret journal documenting his internal resistance to the regime, which his teenaged daughter smuggled out of his flat when it was searched by the Gestapo. Haecker's influence is discernible in the fourth pamphlet, which draws on theology and metaphysics, presenting Hitler as the Antichrist:

> Every word that comes out of Hitler's mouth is a lie. When he says 'peace', he means 'war', and when he blasphemously invokes the name of the Almighty, he means the power of the Evil One, of the fallen angel, of

---

[6] '[E]in Buch, das in dem übelsten Deutsch geschrieben worden ist, das ich je gelesen habe; dennoch ist es von dem Volke der Dichter und Denker zur Bibel erhoben worden'.

Satan. His mouth is the stinking maw of Hell, and his power is, in its very essence, corrupt.[7]

The fourth pamphlet ends with an assurance that the White Rose is not in the pay of a foreign power, before boldly declaring: 'We will not be silent. We are your bad conscience. The White Rose will never leave you in peace!'[8]

Hans and Alex wrote the fourth pamphlet in July 1942. Later that month they and Willi Graf (all medical students conscripted into military service) left Munich for a three-month tour of duty at the Russian front. When they returned, they resumed the pamphlet campaign with Huber now taking an active role. Huber edited the fifth pamphlet in January 1943 based on a draft by Hans. Here there is an even greater sense of urgency: 'HITLER CANNOT WIN THE WAR; HE CAN ONLY PROLONG IT! His guilt and the guilt of his followers continually exceeds all boundaries. Just punishment is nigh!'.[9] Also striking here is the focus on what will happen *after* the war, how Germany will be seen by the rest of the world in the years to come:

---

[7] 'Jedes Wort, das aus Hitlers Munde kommt, ist Lüge. Wenn er Frieden sagt, meint er den Krieg, und wenn er in frevelhaftester Weise den Namen des Allmächtigen nennt, meint er die Macht des Bösen, den gefallenen Engel, den Satan. Sein Mund ist der stinkende Rachen der Hölle, und seine Macht ist im Grunde verworfen'.

[8] 'Wir schweigen nicht, wir sind Euer böses Gewissen; die Weiße Rose lässt Euch keine Ruhe!'.

[9] 'H i t l e r   k a n n   d e n   K r i e g   n i c h t   g e w i n n e n ,   n u r   n o c h   v e r l ä n g e r n ! Seine und seiner Helfer Schuld hat jedes Maß unendlich überschritten. Die gerechte Strafe rückt näher und näher!' (emphasis original).

Germans! [...] Shall we be forever hated and shunned by
the whole world? No! So separate yourselves from the
subhuman nature of National Socialism! Act — prove that
you think differently! A new fight for liberation is at
hand.[10]

Here they take the pejorative word the Nazis used to refer to Jews
and other persecuted groups, 'Untermenschen' ('sub-humans'), and
turn it back round onto the Nazis themselves.

The sixth pamphlet was written by Kurt Huber in February
1943 following the German army's disastrous defeat at Stalingrad.
Huber lays the blame for this squarely at Hitler's door. Unlike the
others, this pamphlet is addressed directly to 'fellow students'
('Kommilitoninnen! Kommilitonen!') and dispenses with the closing
plea to make and distribute further copies. It calls on the students to
rise up and take control of Germany's future:

For us there is only one slogan: fight against the party!
[...] There is no threat that can deter us, not even the
closure of our universities. It is the duty of each and every
one of us to fight for our future, our freedom and honour
in a political system conscious of its own moral
responsibility.[11]

---

[10] 'Deutsche! [...] Sollen wir auf ewig das von aller Welt gehasste und
ausgestoßene Volk sein? Nein! Darum trennt Euch von dem
nationalsozialistischen Untermenschentum! Beweist durch die Tat, dass Ihr
anders denkt! Ein neuer Befreiungskrieg bricht an.'
[11] 'Es gibt für uns nur eine Parole: Kampf gegen die Partei! [...] Kein
Drohmittel kann uns schrecken, auch nicht die Schließung unserer
Hochschulen. Es gilt den Kampf jedes einzelnen von uns um unsere

When the Scholls were arrested in February 1943, Hans had in his pocket the rough version of a seventh pamphlet, drafted by Christoph Probst. He attempted to swallow the incriminating paper but was unable to do so and it was discovered. The sixth pamphlet, however, was smuggled out of the country and in the summer of 1943, millions of copies were dropped by the RAF over Germany. The text bore a new title: 'Manifesto of the Munich Students' ('Manifest der Münchner Studenten'). The same year, the exiled German novelist Thomas Mann dedicated one of his regular BBC broadcasts to the White Rose, declaring: 'Good, marvellous young people! You shall not have died in vain; you shall not be forgotten.'[12] The war would roll on for another two years, but the White Rose would indeed *not* be forgotten.

The members of the White Rose were extraordinary in what they did. Reading their letters and diaries we are confronted with deeply thoughtful and serious individuals, extremely well-read in literature and philosophy. At the same time, they were quite ordinary people. They were also not without a sense of humour. For example, Hans Scholl, in a letter to his parents and sister in March 1942, wondered whether they had received his last letter because the post was very 'irregular'. He adds with more than a hint of mischief:

> I really sympathize with the Gestapo, having to decipher all those different handwritings, some of which are

Zukunft, unsere Freiheit und Ehre in einem seiner sittlichen Verantwortung bewussten Staatswesen.'
[12] 'Brave, herrliche junge Leute! Ihr sollt nicht umsonst gestorben, sollt nicht vergessen sein', Thomas Mann, *Deutsche Hörer! 55 Radiosendungen nach Deutschland von Thomas Mann* (Stockholm: Bermann-Fischer Verlag, 1945), p. 94 (my translation).

highly illegible, but that's what they're paid to do, and duty is duty, gentlemen, isn't it![13]

The story of the White Rose is best told when the group members speak for themselves, in their private writings and in the pamphlets: when they are not idealized or mythologized.

While there are many versions of the pamphlets in English, the White Rose Translation Project set out to produce a new translation with two aims: first, that it should be collaborative; and second, that it should be undertaken by university students. In July 2018 a call for translators was issued among Oxford undergraduates. Applicants were asked to submit a short statement outlining why they would like to be involved, and a translation of an extract from the third pamphlet. Fifteen students from ten colleges were selected to participate and on 12 October 2018 the project was launched. To coincide with this, an exhibition on the White Rose took place in the Voltaire Room at the Taylor Institution Library. 'The White Rose: Reading, Writing, Resistance' presented the group's lives and legacy through examples of what they read and wrote, using books from the Taylorian and Bodleian Library holdings. The annotated catalogue for this exhibition is included at the end of this volume.

---

[13] Hans Scholl, Letter, 18 March 1942, in *At the Heart of the White Rose: Letters and Diaries of Hans and Sophie Scholl*, ed. by Inge Jens, trans. by J. Maxwell Brownjohn (Walden, NY: Plough Publishing House, 2017), p. 217. 'Die Gestapo tut mir wirklich leid, wenn sie diese vielen, zum Teil recht unleserlichen Handschriften entziffern muß, aber sie wird ja dafür bezahlt, und Dienst ist Dienst, nicht wahr, meine Herren!', Hans Scholl and Sophie Scholl, *Briefe und Aufzeichnungen*, ed. by Inge Jens (Frankfurt a.M.: Fischer Taschenbuch Verlag, 1988), p. 101.

The student translators attended an introductory seminar at which we discussed the pamphlets, translation theories, and the aims of our new translation. The students were divided into two groups and two or three students per group took responsibility for one pamphlet. They worked on it together in their own time, then brought a draft version to the next seminar and as a group we discussed the German original and their translation. While I convened the seminars and gave input according to my experience as a university teacher, the students took the lead as 'experts' on their particular pamphlet. The group made suggestions and amendments to these drafts, and they are presented here for the first time. Thus, the students' translations were the result of a truly collaborative process, as indeed the pamphlets themselves were. They outline their approach to the material and translation in the Translators' Introduction.

In addition to the pamphlets, this volume presents five essays about the White Rose which explore in different ways the idea of influences. One of the most persistent questions asked about the members of the White Rose is: just what motivated them to resist Nazism? Paul Shrimpton explores the philosophical, religious, and literary influences on the group. These came not only from texts, but from authors and thinkers the group encountered, such as Carl Muth and Theodor Haecker. Jakob Knab traces Hans Scholl's journey from Hitler Youth leader to spearhead of the resistance, examining the political and cultural encounters that lead him on this journey. Emily Oliver then examines the influence the White Rose may have had during the war by setting out news of the White Rose broadcast in political commentary and features on the BBC German Service. How much was known about the White Rose's actions, and what significance did they have in countering Nazi propaganda? Paul Yowell examines Sophie Scholl's interrogation by the Gestapo agent Robert Mohr as dramatized in Marc Rothemund's 2005 film *Sophie Scholl — Die letzten Tage* (*Sophie Scholl — The Final Days*, 2005). He connects arguments made in the course of the interrogation to philosophical and historical writings about conscience and unjust laws. Finally, Elizabeth M. Ward explores the portrayal of resistance and the figure of Sophie Scholl in Rothemund's *Sophie Scholl — The Final Days*. Ward considers *Sophie Scholl* as an example of an 'historical film', examining, and problematising, its depiction of Sophie and the resistance group. These essays are intended to offer short introductions to those for whom the White Rose is a new subject, and to provide fresh perspectives for those already familiar with the history.

Questions are often asked about the extent to which the White Rose had an 'impact'. There has been criticism of their youthful impetuosity; some have questioned how much concrete change they really achieved. Hildegard Kronawitter, of the White Rose Foundation in Munich, addresses these points in her foreword to this book. As Annette Dumbach and Jud Newborn write, 'The impact of the White Rose cannot be measured in tyrants destroyed, regimes overthrown, justice restored. A scale with another dimension is needed, and then their significance is deeper; it goes even beyond the Third Reich, beyond Germany'.[14] Their story gives us hope, and especially for those of us who work closely with young

---

[14] Annette Dumnbach and Jud Newborn, *Sophie Scholl and the White Rose* (Oxford: Oneworld Publications, 2007), p. 185.

people, it provides a moving and inspiring example of how conscience and moral courage can challenge injustice.

Dr Alexandra Lloyd is Lecturer in German at St Edmund Hall and Magdalen College, Oxford. Her main research interests lie in twentieth-century literature and film, particularly cultural memories of childhood, war, and dictatorship. She leads the White Rose Project, a research and outreach initiative telling the story of the White Rose in the UK.

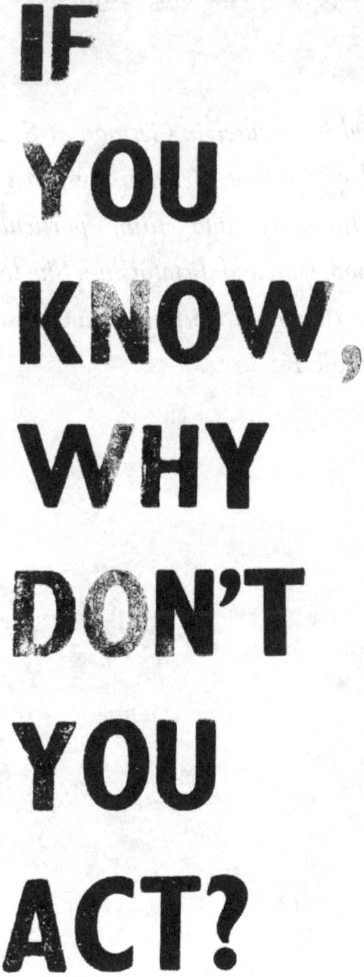

IF YOU KNOW, WHY DON'T YOU ACT?

Figure 1. Poster designed and printed by student translators at the Bodleian's Bibliographical Press in preparation for the exhibition 'White Rose: Writing and Resistance', held in the Bodleian Library Proscholium between May and July 2019.

AT THE HEART OF THE WHITE ROSE — CULTURAL AND RELIGIOUS INFLUENCES ON THE MUNICH STUDENTS

Paul Shrimpton

Confronted with the extraordinary deeds of heroism of the White Rose students, it is natural to ask where they acquired their deep convictions, their strength of character, their fearlessness in action. Of course we will never know their inner thoughts, but we can at least trace many of the ways in which they were influenced in the rich trail of letters and diaries[1] they left behind them; we can also learn from the Gestapo interrogation records and court proceedings,[2] though clearly these have to be treated with caution. From all this we can assemble a coherent picture of the lives of the White Rose students and identify the main influences on them: from family and culture; from school, youth groups and church; and from friends, older guides and mentors.

---

[1] The most significant collection is *Hans Scholl, Sophie Scholl: Briefe und Aufzeichnungen*, ed. by Inge Jens (Frankfurt a.M.: Fischer, 1984) which appeared in translation as *At the Heart of the White Rose: Letters and Diaries of Hans and Sophie Scholl*, ed. by Inge Jens and trans. by J. Maxwell Brownjohn (New York: Harper & Row, 1987).
[2] The Gestapo destroyed most of their files at the end of the war, but around 60,000 survived, including the White Rose ones.

But we need to tread carefully. It is not easy for us to imagine ourselves in the moral chaos of Nazi Germany and to appreciate the overwhelming pressure to compromise one's conscience and settle for an easy life; only a tiny minority had the courage and conviction to withstand that pressure.

Hans and Sophie Scholl were the second and fourth of five children, and were encouraged by their parents to read widely and to develop an interest in music, art and the outdoor life. Like most other youngsters, they were inspired by Hitler's talk of helping the Fatherland achieve greatness and prosperity, and were swept along by feelings of comradeship engendered by the uniforms, songs and marching of the Hitler Youth. They even defied their father, a pacifist, by joining when membership was voluntary, and became group leaders. But over time, as Hans and Sophie experienced the increasing conformism of school and the growing militarisation of the Hitler Youth, they became disenchanted. For Hans, ironically, the defining moment occurred at the 1935 Nuremburg Rally, which he attended as a flag-bearer. Thereafter the Scholl household became a magnet for kindred spirits who felt disillusioned or alienated, a place of sanctuary where the children could talk openly to trusted friends and relatives. They read banned books and criticised the regime at meal-times; Herr Scholl, who had always been vehemently anti-Nazi, would sometimes leave the table early, saying, 'Now, if you'll excuse me, I'll go and earn a jail sentence' — his joking euphemism for listening to forbidden radio stations such as the BBC or the Swiss Beromünster.[3]

While Hans and Sophie were raised by Frau Scholl as Bible-reading Lutherans, Alex Schmorell and Willi Graf had very different religious backgrounds. Alex, born to a German father and a Russian mother, was brought up Russian Orthodox; his first language was always Russian and he felt at home in the world of Pushkin, Gogol and Dostoyevsky. Despite being a German national, he avoided joining the Hitler Youth, and when called up for military service he refused to take the oath of loyalty to Hitler; nevertheless, he had to serve in the *Wehrmacht*.

Willi Graf was raised as a devout Catholic and joined the Catholic youth group *Neudeutschland* (New Germany). When Hitler came to power, he made a list of all his friends and crossed out those who had joined the Hitler Youth; in 1934 he joined a new underground youth group, the *Grauer Orden* (Grey Order), but it lasted four years before being closed down. When he began his medical studies at the University of Bonn, he had to combine them with placements in field hospitals in the Balkans, Poland and Russia; there he witnessed the unspeakable brutality of his fellow-soldiers, fuelling his hatred for National Socialism.

In the summer of 1941 the Catholic bishop of Münster, Clemens von Galen, took the momentous decision to speak out from the pulpit against Nazi policies. In three sermons he deplored their

---

[3] Named after its transmitter at Beromünster, Swiss national radio was the only German-language platform for public criticism of Nazi ideology, once the Nazi regime had brought the German and Austrian press into line.

'deep-seated hatred of Christianity, which they are determined to destroy',[4] and condemned the Nazi policy of euthanasia, the 'monstrous doctrine, which tries to justify the murder of the innocent, which permits the slaughter of invalids who are no longer capable of work, cripples, the incurable, the aged and the infirm', opening the way to the murder of all 'unproductive people'.[5] It was the first time that the regime had been challenged so publicly, and it caused a sensation. Copies of the sermons were sent anonymously to homes all over the country, with the plea to make copies and pass them on. Hans was deeply impressed by this act of opposition; he told his sister Inge, 'Finally a man has had the courage to speak out'.[6] The copying and circulation of von Galen's sermons (which Sophie did secretly) gave him the idea of using pamphlets as a way of expressing non-violent opposition to the regime which would be hard for the Gestapo to trace.

Hans, Sophie, Alex and Willi were all voracious readers, whether at school or university or on Labour Service assignments. For them, books were food for the mind, as well as a way to explore the world and themselves. Later their reading became a means to make sense of the turmoil around them and enabled them to see that the National Socialist system had forfeited its claim to the allegiance of its citizens. They wrote to each other about their reading, and

---

[4] Clemens von Galen, sermon preached at the Liebfrauenkirche, Münster on 20 July 1941.
[5] Clemens von Galen, sermon preached at St Lambert's, Münster on 3 August 1941.
[6] Inge Scholl, *The White Rose: Munich, 1942–1943* (Middletown: Wesleyan University Press USA, 1983), p. 20. See also Inge Scholl, *Die Weiße Rose* (Frankfurt a.M.: Verlag der Frankfurter Hefte, 1952).

passed on books. When Sophie went skiing with some of her siblings and family friends at Christmas 1940, they read aloud by candlelight *Journal d'un curé de campagne* (*The Diary of a Country Priest*, 1936), George Bernanos's (banned) novel; both grittily down-to-earth and profoundly spiritual at once, it was written to help Christians 'digest' the modern world and experience a foretaste of heaven in the very ugliness and sorrow of this world. The following year, when Hans was able to join the ski party, they read Dostoyevsky's *The Double* (1846).

During the first two years of the war Hans and Sophie developed a growing interest in philosophy and theology, which became for them an alternative world to fascist National Socialism. In their search of meaning they stumbled on Christian writers, ancient and modern, and there discovered answers to their deepest longings. They began discussing the big questions of life which had been brought home to them by the events unfolding across Europe. They both detested regimentation and reacted against being herded into camps by assuming a state of continuous internal resistance. Feeling abandoned in an alien world and finding that the conflict was unbearable when they were separated from friends and family, they sought out solitude and turned to prayer. Books, especially forbidden ones, came to play an even more important part in their lives. Favourite authors included several members of *Renouveau Catholique*,[7] the philosophical, socio-critical and literary movement arising at the end of the nineteenth century.

---

[7] Besides Bernanos, others who formed part of the movement were Léon Bloy, Paul Claudel, André Gide, Julien Green, Francis Jammes and François Mauriac — all of whom were on Hans' reading list.

Hans met Alex and Willi while studying medicine at the Ludwig Maximillian University in Munich. They were part-students, part-soldiers: medical students during term-time, medical assistants in field hospitals in vacations. The medical corps turned out to be an ideal place to meet pacifists, fellow dissidents and opponents of the regime, and to exchange ideas and banned literature. Hans and Alex set up a book-reading group among their friends, and they chose *Le soulier de satin* (*The Satin Slipper*, 1929), often considered the masterpiece of the poet-dramatist Paul Claudel; books like this could only be obtained under the counter from second-hand bookshops. The two soldier-medics developed a deep friendship, and in this way Hans was introduced to contemporary Russian authors such as Nikolai Berdyaev, who had abandoned Marxism for mystical Christianity. During one period of intense medical training, while attending forty hours of lectures a week, Hans managed to read in succession Hans Carossa's *Das Jahr der schönen Täuschungen* (*The Year of Sweet Illusions*, 1941), a novel based on the author's days as a medical student; Pascal's *Pensées* (1670); Charles Baudelaire's *Les fleurs du mal* (*The Flowers of Evil*, 1857); Dante's *Divina commedia* (*Divine Comedy*, 1320); and Etienne Gilson's *Introduction à l'étude de Saint Augustin* (*The Christian Philosophy of Saint Augustine*, 1929).

The students also drew inspiration from dissident academics and anti-Nazi intellectuals. Like the students, these cultural dissidents formed their own support networks; and when the two groups — students and academics — came together, each benefitted from the presence of the other. Alex and Hans occasionally attended an underground cultural reading group which Alex's father ran, but the most influential group they joined was coordinated by the Catholic journalist Carl Muth, founder and editor of the journal *Hochland*

(*Highland*), the leading magazine — with a circulation of around 12,000 — of intellectual resistance to Nazi ideology. Their encounter with Muth opened a window onto another world, as he introduced them to scholars and writers who were vehemently opposed to National Socialism, and it also affected a remarkable religious awakening in Hans, Sophie and their friends.

But Muth was not just an entrée to a circle of dissidents; he had a talent for teaching and dealing with young people. The support Muth had given to hearts and minds in the face of Nazi ideology was not stifled by the suppression of *Hochland* in 1941; he simply diverted his energies to the Scholls and their student friends. He conversed with them, lent them books, tutored them in theology, and introduced them to other writers and thinkers. In turn, this younger generation helped Muth not to lose hope that the German people would regain its conscience; for him they represented a 'secret Germany' who could uphold and pass on the values he cherished and had made his life's work. When Sophie arrived in Munich in May 1942 to begin her university studies, she stayed with Muth until she found her own lodgings. Hans, meanwhile, had agreed to reorganise and catalogue Muth's vast private library, stocked largely with banned books.

The four White Rose leaflets that were composed, duplicated and distributed by Alex and Hans in the period 27 June –11 July 1942 drew from their meetings with Muth's close friends, above all with the philosopher Theodor Haecker, effectively one of the sponsors of the White Rose students. Forbidden to publish or speak in public, Haecker had come to regard the Second World War as a war about truth, and believed that National Socialism sought to impose itself as an alternative religion to Christianity. After discovering the writings of John Henry Newman,[8] from 1920 till his death in 1945 he devoted himself to translating Newman into German. As Haecker was Hans's most important guide at the time, he was influential in shaping the style and content of the leaflets. Expressions such as 'the stinking maw of Hell' ('stinkende[r] Rachen der Hölle') and 'atheistic war machine' ('atheistische Kriegsmachine') in the first leaflet, 'ceaseless deception' ('die stete Lüge') and the 'meaning of our history' ('Sinn unserer Geschichte') in the second, and 'dictatorship of evil' ('Diktatur des Bösen') and 'spawn of Hell' ('Ausgeburt der Hölle') in the third, were all phrases culled or adapted from Haecker's journal,[9] and they indicate that Hans had adopted his mentor's prophetic opposition to the regime.

The fourth leaflet was written the day after Haecker had spoken to a circle of friends gathered by Alex and Hans. During this long evening meeting, Haecker drew from Kierkegaard and Newman in his attempt to discern the metaphysical background of the war. Willi recorded in his diary that Haecker read from his theology of history, *Der Christ und die Geschichte* (*The Christian and History*, 1935), in which he examines the role of divine providence

---

[8] John Henry Newman was an undergraduate at Trinity College, Oxford (1817–20) and a Fellow of Oriel (1822–45). He was vicar of the University Church of St Mary the Virgin (1828–43) and (unofficial) leader of the Tractarian or Oxford Movement.

[9] Published in 1947 as *Tag- und Nachtbücher*, it is now recognised as an exceptionally profound reflection on fascism and on an intellectual's interior resistance to it. It was first published in English as *Journal in the Night* (London: Harvill Press, 1949).

in time.[10] He developed his ideas on fallen angels and pure spirits, on good and evil, Christ and the Antichrist, God and the devil, on the liar's false image of human nature, and on the appearance of the Antichrist in person in the last days of history.[11] Haecker also read from his journal: many of his entries confirmed Hans in his understanding of events and the need for the White Rose leaflets to point the way for others. Evidently, he absorbed from Haecker the conviction that Germany's apostasy could pave the way for the Antichrist, or at least his shadow. The impulsive and spirited Hans took up this cluster of apocalyptic images and used it to draw up the fourth leaflet.

From late July to early November 1942 Alex, Hans and Willi served on the Russian front. Sickened by what they witnessed there, they returned to Munich determined to write more leaflets and this time to distribute them in their thousands across Germany and Austria, while at the same time linking up with other resistance groups. They often met up at concerts or wine bars before returning to their lodgings to conduct their resistance business. They also continued to meet with Muth's friends. On 13 December 1942 Haecker brought to a meeting his draft translation of Newman's four Advent sermons on 'The Patristical Idea of Antichrist',[12] the pivotal

---

[10] The relevant passage from *The Christian and History* is reproduced in *Die Weiße Rose: Student Resistance to National Socialism, 1942–1943*, ed. by Hinrich Siefken (Nottingham: University of Nottingham, 1991), pp. 165–66.

[11] Willi Graf, *Briefe und Aufzeichnungen*, ed. by Anneliese Knoop-Graf and Inge Jens (Frankfurt a.M.: Fischer, 1994), p. 41.

[12] Besides being included in the series 'Tracts for the Times' as Tract 83, the sermons were published as part of *Discussion and Arguments* (London:

text for Haecker's thesis about Christianity in the Third Reich. To judge from diary entries and letters of those present, it was a life-changing occasion for them. But not for Hans; he disagreed with Haecker, insisting that the Antichrist *had* come, and was none other than Hitler, and that he must be overthrown by the German resistance. The next (and last) two leaflets he and Alex produced no longer bore the name 'White Rose' (though historians call them White Rose leaflets), but simply spoke of resistance.

The White Rose students who were executed in 1943 were hungry for answers that might explain the nightmare they found themselves living through. Newman was one of the Christian sages who was able to respond to their need to make sense of the cultural and moral chaos around them. Having originally sought answers in Nietzsche, they turned to St Augustine, then St Thomas Aquinas and Pascal, for an adequate response and guidance on how to act under a regime governed by unjust laws. The arguments that Sophie articulated under interrogation by the Gestapo — accurately recorded in transcripts that were used to brilliant effect in the 2005 film *Sophie Scholl — Die letzten Tage* (*Sophie Scholl — The Final Days*)[13] — show how thoroughly the students had thought through some of the most difficult questions of modern times.

When Sophie's boyfriend, a *Luftwaffe* officer called Fritz Hartnagel, was deployed to the Eastern Front in 1942, Sophie's parting gift to him was two volumes of Newman's sermons.

Longman, Green & Co., 1872; 1907), pp. 44–108. Haecker's translation of the four sermons was published posthumously.
[13] This was the third film about the White Rose and was nominated for an Oscar in the category Best Foreign Language Film.

Witnessing the carnage in Russia, he wrote to Sophie to say that reading Newman's words in such an awful place was like tasting 'drops of precious wine'.[14] In another letter he wrote: 'we know by whom we were created and that we stand in a relationship of moral obligation to our creator. Conscience gives us the capacity to distinguish between good and evil'[15] — words taken almost verbatim from a sermon of Newman's called 'The Testimony of Conscience'.[16] In this sermon Newman explains that conscience is an echo of the voice of God enlightening each person to moral truth in concrete situations. All of us, he argues, have a duty to obey a good conscience over and above all other considerations. It would not be too far-fetched to suggest that the final words of the fourth leaflet might have been written under the influence of the Oxford clergyman-academic: 'We will not be silent. We are your bad conscience. The White Rose will never leave you in peace! Please duplicate and re-distribute!'.

Dr Paul Shrimpton teaches at Magdalen College School, Oxford and is a specialist in the history of education. Besides two books on John Henry Newman, he has published 'Conscience before Conformity: Hans and Sophie Scholl and the White Rose Resistance in Nazi Germany' (2018).

---

[14] Fritz Hartnagel to Sophie Scholl, 26 June 1942, cited in Dermot Fenlon, 'From the White Star to the Red Rose: J. H. Newman and the Conscience of the State', *Internationale Cardinal-Newman Studien* 20 (2010), 45–73 (p. 63).

[15] Fritz Hartnagel to Sophie Scholl, 4 July 1942, cited in Fenlon, 'White Star to the Red Rose', p. 63.

[16] John Henry Newman, *Plain and Parochial Sermons* V (London: Longmans, Green & Co, 1840; 1907), pp. 237–53.

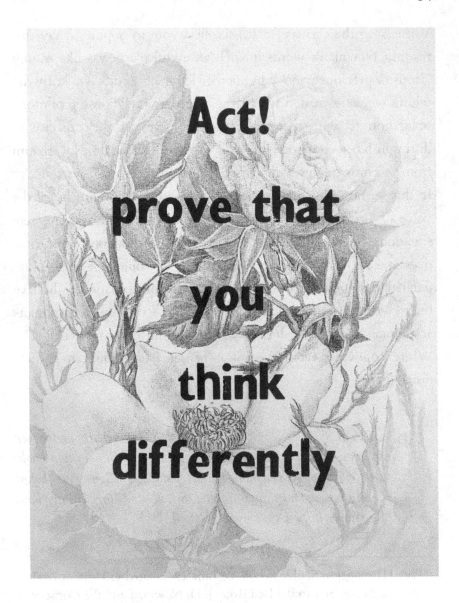

Figure 2. Poster designed and printed by student translators at the Bodleian's Bibliographical Press.

DIE WEISSE ROSE:
FREEDOM OF CONSCIENCE OVER
TOTALITARIAN CONFORMITY

Jakob Knab

Hans Scholl was the political and charismatic head of the White Rose. Accordingly, the primary focus of the following article will be Scholl's search for the meaning of human existence, and his longing for free space and liberty, in the midst of a totalitarian regime.

The Nazi dictatorship was successful in cowing its populace. Adaptation, as a necessary means of survival, and paralysing fear were the consequences; resistance to the totalitarian regime could only take place underground. In view of the apathy and passivity of the majority of the German population at that time, Hans Scholl remains, even today, a remarkable example of courage and the desire for freedom. With ever-increasing autonomy, he defied the influence of propaganda, remaining intellectually independent in the face of enforced totalitarian conformity.

Analysis of the White Rose reveals once again that the history of liberty rests on the creative force of a minority of extraordinary individuals: the conscientious struggle for truth must inevitably come into conflict with the demands of totalitarian rule. In opposing the racism and militarism of the Nazi regime, and echoing Paul's Epistle to the Romans, Sophie Scholl maintained in October 1942

'Yes, we too believe in the triumph of the stronger — but of the stronger in spirit'.[1]

A Sergeant in the Medical Corps

Hans Scholl came to Munich in April 1939 to pursue a course in medicine at the city's university. The young men in his circle there were uniformed medical students, and from April 1941, they were each assigned to newly-founded student medical divisions. Scholl, Schmorell and Willi Graf were posted as sergeants to the 2nd Student Company of the Munich Army Medical Squadron. While on service, their daily activities consisted of 'pointless roll-calls', as Hans Scholl would describe it, in addition to drills, watch duties, air defence and political instruction. Following the outbreak of war in 1939, the academic calendar was reorganised into a system of three terms per year: medical students were to be fast-tracked through their degrees. For Scholl, the tensions between the regimented daily life of the barracks and the freedoms afforded by his studies began to weigh increasingly heavily. The core value of liberty plays a decisive role in his letters and notes from this period. Now 24, he began to seek refuge in non-conformist behaviour, whilst also attempting to withdraw physically from his surroundings. He was soon refusing — despite tightened regulations — to sleep in his allotted 18-man dormitory in the auxiliary accommodation at Munich's Bergmann School. Later, in March 1942, during a clinical traineeship at the St. Ottilien Military Reserve Hospital (near Landsberg am Lech), he

---

[1] 'Ja, wir glauben auch an den Sieg der Stärkeren, aber der Stärkeren im Geiste', Sophie Scholl, Letter to Fritz Hartnagel, 28 October 1942, in *Hans Scholl und Sophie Scholl: Briefe und Aufzeichnungen*, ed. by Inge Jens (Frankfurt a.M.: Fischer, 1984), p. 224.

ruffled feathers significantly by letting his hair grow longer than rules permitted.

Scholl suffered equally under the constraints of regimented military service and amidst the mindless barking of orders during the roll-calls on the parade ground. He was repulsed by the drills, and by the procedures to which he was daily subjected as a soldier. Each morning, he was sickened and revolted by senseless parades. Nor could he be reconciled to the strict ordinances applied to his unit in the barracks. On one occasion, during a lecture, the laughter of several students exposed an academic to ridicule, a teacher whose expertise in the subject was unremarkable, but who made mindless public show of his staunch Nazi sympathies. When, in a response at the end of January, the company commander announced sanctions during a roll-call at the lecture theatre, he was himself booed in turn by a number of students. There were interrogations and denunciations as a consequence. The company was collectively punished in February 1942, and confined to quarters for four weeks. Hans Scholl saw himself as a 'prisoner of the state' ('Gefangener des Staates'),[2] pilloried and imprisoned for a 'trivial offence'.

Such privileged student companies were no bastion of liberty, however, nor a hotbed of resistance. With the exception of the circle of friends surrounding the White Rose, which was active outside the student company in any case, there was no noteworthy opposition among these units. By February 1942, the atmosphere in the Munich Student Company had become so toxic — the consequence of an incident whose details are unknown — that Hans

---

[2] Hans Scholl, Letter to his sister Elisabeth, 10 February 1942, in *Briefe und Aufzeichnungen*, p. 78.

Scholl could write with repulsion of a 'culture of informers of the most despicable sort'. At the same time, Scholl cultivated contacts with members of his company who shared his sentiments, and who had, like him, established a critical distance from the regime. Among them was the medical sergeant Josef Gieles, who had himself developed spaces of intellectual freedom by reading the works of John Henry Newman.[3]

The World of the Mind as a Space of Liberty and Protection

During his search for meaning, for personal identity and a philosophy of life, Hans Scholl made the acquaintance of Carl Muth, the editor of the Catholic monthly *Hochland*, in August 1941. Some months previously, when the Wehrmacht attacked the Soviet Union in June, Muth's magazine had been forced to shut down on account of 'war-related paper shortages' (as it was officially termed). Noteworthy theologians, cultural philosophers and writers of the time had written critical articles for *Hochland*, attacking Nazi ideology as a false doctrine of salvation. The scholar Theodor Haecker had contributed to the magazine German translations of the sermons of John Henry Newman. Their central theme was the

---

[3] Josef Gieles, Letter to his parents, 11 June 1941: 'Gekauft habe ich zwei Bücher von Kardinal Newman. Ich habe in einem angefangen und bin begeistert und hingerissen wie noch selten von einem Buch. Es sind Aufsätze "Kirche und Wissenschaft" (*Idea of a University*) anlässlich der Gründung einer katholischen Universität. Seine Gedankengänge sind äußerst klar, prägnant, der Stil glänzend, der Inhalt zeugt von einem Feuergeist, wie es selten einen gibt. Sein Katholizismus ist vorbildlich und es tut einem mal unendlich gut in der jetzigen Zeit, solche Gedankengänge zu lesen.' Heinrich Kanz (ed.), *Der studentische Freundeskreis der Weißen Rose: Ausgewählte Brief- und Tagebuchauszüge* (Frankfurt a.M.: Peter Lang, 2011), p. 172.

conflict between freedom of conscience and the encroachment of worldly authorities. They called for a steadfast stance against the impositions of authoritarianism, and for the freedom of conscience of individuals over the coercions and pretensions to power of authorities, giving rise to the idea that all evil in the course of human history is ultimately overcome through the martyrdom of the faithful. In the middle of January 1942, a reading group met one evening in Muth's home. Although the Nazi regime had enacted a ban on Haecker's speeches and publications, he presented some of Newman's sermons and read from the volume *The Mystery of the Holy Trinity and the Incarnation* (1940). Hans Scholl must surely have felt that he was being personally addressed, hearing this English theologian talking of the Christian confession of faith, while still keeping in mind the emotions, morale, imagination and conscience of believers.

Since Theodor Haecker visited Carl Muth, his close confidante, every fortnight in the Munich neighbourhood of Solln, it was perhaps inevitable that he should make the acquaintance of Hans Scholl in person. The young student was fascinated by Haecker's charisma. For all that Haecker was often seen as reserved and aloof, their common rejection of National Socialism nevertheless led to a mutual understanding between the two men.

Haecker's influence, particularly on the fourth pamphlet of the 12th July 1942, is borne out by the fact that he had presented extracts from his work *The Christian and History* (*Der Christ und die Geschichte*) to his friends, during a reading group in Munich on the evening of the 10th. That night, Haecker had referred to the motifs of the 'fallen angel' and 'pure spirits', to 'Christ and the Antichrist', to 'good and evil', to 'God and the Devil', to the 'mendacious falsification of the true being of Man', and to the 'appearance of the Antichrist in the flesh during the last days of history'. That evening, moreover, Haecker read from texts that would be published later, in the postwar period, under the title *Journal in the Night* (*Tag- und Nachtbücher 1939–1945*). There, he wrote of the Nazi regime that

> They have gained all their successes and all their victories
> to date under the sign of the Antichrist, and you would
> have us believe that they do not persecute Christ? Those
> who still seek to convince us of this are no longer even
> idiots, but rather hypocrites.[4]

There is much to suggest that Hans Scholl, by inclination eager as he was, took up these motifs and composed the fourth pamphlet directly under their influence: Haecker's characteristically apocalyptic tone is palpable. The pamphlet was distributed two days later, on the 12th July 1942, and argued that against the 'metaphysical backdrop of the war' ('den metaphysischen Hintergrund dieses Krieges'), the 'power of evil' ('die Macht des Bösen'), the 'fallen angel', 'Satan', the 'demons', and the 'Antichrist' held sway. On the other side, it asserted, was Man's acknowledgment of the 'name of the Almighty'.

In the spring of 1942, Scholl created a private Christian world by cultivating a personal relationship with the monasteries. He found himself drawn to those libraries where, even after the book- burnings

---

[4] 'Sie haben bis jetzt alle ihre Erfolge und alle ihre Siege im Zeichen des Antichrist errungen, und ihr wollt glauben, daß sie Christus nicht verfolgen. Wer uns das noch einreden will, der ist nicht einmal mehr ein Dummkopf, der ist ein Heuchler.' Theodor Haecker, *Tag- und Nachtbücher 1939-1945*, ed. by Hinrich Siefken, Brenner-Studien, 9 (Innsbruck: Haymon, 1989), p. 178 [Notat 786].

of May 1933 and the 'cleansing' of public libraries, the literary heritage of the Christian West was still safeguarded. Scholl consequently sought out and maintained contacts with the 'library Fathers' among the Benedictines. At Muth's personal recommendation, Scholl also made the acquaintance of the Benedictine monk Dom Romuald Bauerreiß, who belonged to St. Boniface's Abbey in Munich. In spring 1942, Muth asked Dom Romuald to receive his protégé Hans Scholl and the latter's friend Alexander Schmorell. The two friends were delighted by the quiet and intellectually stimulating atmosphere of the foundation's library, magnificent and steeped in history as it was, and regarded as a miniature cathedral of the spirit. There, together with Schmorell, Scholl studied works of great theologians, among them the Dominican Saint Thomas Aquinas and his reflections on the justification of tyrannicide.

During the so-called 'storming of the monasteries' in spring 1941, over 200 Catholic abbeys and monasteries on Reich territory had been sequestered by the Gestapo. This was a step in the preparation of the planned offensive against the USSR, as the monastic establishments were transformed into military hospitals for the care of the wounded. There were now fears of a total dissolution of St. Boniface's Abbey in the heart of Munich. Seeing the library in such danger, Hans Scholl asked: 'Father, do you really want to abandon your beautiful library to the Nazis?'. In order to preserve the most valuable books from the foundation's library, Scholl and Schmorell, together with Dom Romuald, began an effort to save them. They succeeded in taking 200 precious and unique volumes back to the Munich borough of Harlaching (where Schmorell's father had a doctor's practice), stashing them in rucksacks they had brought on the way.

It was again thanks to Carl Muth that Hans Scholl met other figures from the intellectual world. At the beginning of June 1942, in a house by the English Garden near the University, a group of around twenty educated citizens, critics of the regime, met for an evening of reading and conversation. Their talk revolved around such guiding principles as 'internal conversion'. On the 17th June 1942, when Hans Scholl had been invited to another meeting of these anti-regime academics, he first came into closer acquaintance with Professor Kurt Huber. The genteel and well-educated hostess of the evening had begun by reading personal reflections on 'religious renewal'. A heated exchange then followed on how best to combat the destruction of 'internal principles', as was then being carried out by Hitler's regime. Kurt Huber's outraged words have been passed down to us, his demand that 'We have to do something — and we have to do it now!' ('Man muss etwas tun, und zwar heute noch!').[5] It was likely in this moment that the spark caught in Hans Scholl, eager and hungry for action, and he was seized by Kurt Huber's impassioned appeal.

The *Volksempfänger* — 'Enemy Stations' — 'Broadcasting Crimes'

The *Volksempfänger* ('people's receiver') was a radio set, developed at the behest of Reich Minister of Propaganda Joseph Goebbels and

---

[5] Cited in *Wider die Kriegsmaschinerie: Kriegserfahrungen und Motive des Widerstandes der Weißen Rose*, ed. by Detlef Bald (Essen: Klartext Verlag, 2005), p. 124.

introduced a few months after Hitler's seizure of power at the end of January 1933. It has been viewed as one of the most important instruments of Nazi propaganda. For this reason, in a regulation on extraordinary broadcasts at the beginning of the Second World War, Goebbels implemented the threat of draconian punishments, including the death penalty, for listening to 'enemy stations' — particularly the German-language service of the BBC in London.

The *Volksempfänger* thus became one of the most important propaganda tools of the National Socialist government, broadcasting Hitler's speeches, reinterpreting the details of losses and defeats as victories after the tide of the war had turned, and testifying to the willingness of the German people to make sacrifices. As the reality of bombing raids and high casualties (particularly on the Eastern Front) became ever-more at odds with the content of the programmes, however, rumours began to spread, consensus began to crumble, and the credibility of Nazi war propaganda began to wane. Hans Scholl's home was among those that listened to so-called 'enemy stations', and his father, Robert Scholl, faced trial in August 1942 for supposed 'broadcasting crimes'. He had been denounced for calling Hitler a 'scourge of God'; Thomas Mann had previously used this term for Hitler in a radio address of December 1941.[6]

In May 1942, Thomas Mann had attacked National Socialism as a 'regiment of scoundrels' and had spoken of Hitler's 'lying words'. He had also expressed his hope that the German people would pass judgement on this 'clique of criminals', as it had been 'corrupted and

---

[6] See also Martina Hoffschulte, *'Deutsche Hörer!' Thomas Manns Rundfunkreden (1940 bis 1945) im Werkkontext, mit einem Anhang: Quellen und Materialien* (Münster: Telos, 2004).

abused'. In prophetic style, Mann appealed to the German people to 'set an example' and 'after long aberrations, to lead a new, respectable existence'. Barely a month later, at the close of June 1942, Scholl and Schmorell composed their first pamphlet, with the first sentence reading: 'Complicity with the "governance" of an irresponsible clique of rulers driven by their darkest urges, and complicity without resistance — nothing is more unworthy of a civilised people.'[7] We may assume that Mann's radio address of May 1942 had given Scholl and Schmorell the final impetus to rebel against the deceptive and repressive regime, and thus to compose their leaflets. Mann's remarks on Hitler's 'lying words' are echoed in the fourth pamphlet, where we find the accusation that 'every word that comes out of Hitler's mouth is a lie' ('Jedes Wort, das aus Hitlers Munde kommt, ist Lüge').

When, in June 1942, Hans Scholl and Alexander Schmorell decided to carry out their leaflet campaign, they assumed that German defeat and the end of the war would come soon. Reports of this kind from British propaganda were familiar to them through their illicit consumption of foreign radio stations. The war had reached the period when the so-called 'Greater German Reich', together with its ally Italy, was at the apex of its territorial extent — from the Atlantic coast of France to the military front in the USSR, from Leningrad via Stalingrad to the Caucasus, and from the North Cape of Norway to the Mediterranean coast of Africa.

The very first pamphlet makes reference to the devastating bombing raids on Cologne. In the first attack on the city, on the

---

[7] 'Nichts ist eines Kulturvolkes unwürdiger, als sich ohne Widerstand von einer verantwortungslosen und dunklen Trieben ergebenen Herrscherclique "regieren" zu lassen.'

night of the 30th-31st May 1942, the RAF had deployed over 1,000 bombers simultaneously, under the codename 'Operation Millennium'. British propaganda portrayed this operation as a turning point in the Second World War. And from exile, Mann addressed the educated classes of the German Reich. Between October 1940 and May 1945, in a series of radio addresses entitled *German Listeners!*, the BBC in London broadcast his dispatches once per month; 58 were transmitted in total. Through these addresses, Mann pursued the aim of calling his German listeners to resistance against Hitler and National Socialism.

Conclusion

The history of opposition to the Nazi regime remains a challenge for the generations that followed it. Understanding it demands a high level of historical awareness, political education and ethical judgement. Those who are occupied with the resistance to Hitler must seek to answer these questions: why were people like them — in contrast to the multitudes of fellow travellers, loyal henchmen, and willing excutioners — themselves prepared and able to make a stand and resist this 'dictatorship of evil'? From what sources did they derive their inner strength? What values, traditions and visions guided them, making them the spiritually and morally stronger party in the struggle against the National Socialists? How did they attain such faculty of judgement?

In the case of Hans Scholl, the following motives take precedence: as a young man with a great thirst for knowledge, he remained always open and responsive to all things true, good and beautiful. As a student of medicine and a prospective doctor, he was moved by the unutterable pain of the victims, and by the suffering and horrors of the war. In his search for meaning, he discovered the Christian faith and developed clear-sighted ideas on what was truly good and what was radically evil. His energetic personality constantly sought spaces of freedom, both individually and politically. He risked his young life in the resistance to Hitler's tyranny, fighting for human dignity and freedom of conscience. In today's Germany, the friends of the White Rose serve as icons of opposition to Nazi dictatorship. Scholl's final cry, 'long live freedom!' ('Es lebe die Freiheit!'), may initially have been in vain — but it was never meaningless.

Translated by Samuel Thompson

Jakob Knab worked in secondary education for many years, latterly as a 'Studiendirektor'. He studied English and Catholic Theology in Munich and Linguistics at Edinburgh, and completed his postgraduate studies in the Philosophy of Religion at Christ Church, Oxford. He has spoken and published widely on the politics of history, the maintenance of traditions, and the culture of remembrance. His biographic work 'Ich schweige nicht. Hans Scholl und die Weiße Rose' ('I won't be Silenced: Hans Scholl and the White Rose') was published in 2018 by the Wissenschaftliche Buchgesellschaft in Darmstadt.

Samuel Thompson is a PhD student at King's College London, working under the London Arts and Humanities Partnership. He completed his undergraduate studies in Classics and German, and a master's degree in German, at Magdalen College, Oxford. His current research examines the reception of Classical antiquity in German exile literature between 1933 and 1945. His academic interests include Classical Reception more broadly, in addition to cultural opposition to Nazism, memory culture and Austrian literature.

'Deutsche Hörer!' News of the White Rose on the BBC German Service*

Emily Oliver

What could Germans have known about the activities of the White Rose group during the war? What kind of influence might this resistance group have had on Germans far beyond Munich, living under a regime of state-controlled media? One important (though illegal) channel of information available to those in the Third Reich was the BBC German Service, broadcasting in German from London. Following the executions of Hans Scholl, Sophie Scholl, and Christoph Probst, from mid-April to late June 1943 the German Service repeatedly referred to the activities of White Rose members. Examining the ways in which the different broadcasts engaged with the resistance group demonstrates the importance of these narratives for countering official Nazi propaganda.

Founded in response to the Munich crisis in 1938, the BBC German Service sought to gain listeners by providing truthful information on the war. The key element at the heart of all programming was accurate and up-to-date news, acting as 'the magnet which attracted the audience'.[1] Other formats included talks,

* This work was funded by the Leverhulme Trust through a Leverhulme Early Career Fellowship. All translations are my own unless otherwise indicated.

music, and satirical features, all of which were to act as 'a vehicle for propaganda' and 'bait for the news'.[2] Under the leadership of Hugh Carleton Greene (brother of novelist Graham Greene), the German Service assembled a highly diverse workforce: some were British citizens with excellent language skills, others were Jewish émigrés from German-speaking countries. This balance of British nationals and foreigners was necessary, since Germans and Austrians were banned from voicing opinions on the air: although they could write commentaries, these had to be delivered by British staff members. The German Service's key objective was

> to break down the will to fight of the German people by convincing them that defeat is certain, but that defeat at the hands of the Allies would not have intolerable consequences for the ordinary citizen. In short [...] to provide a judicious blend of 'despair' and 'hope' propaganda.[3]

The stylistic implications of this were a calm, measured delivery by all speakers to contrast with the hectoring sounds of Nazi broadcasts. In order to persuade its German audience to take the considerable risk of listening to enemy broadcasts, the German Service judiciously differentiated between warmongering Nazis and supposedly

---

[1] 'BBC German Service' (25 March 1942), E1/758/2, BBC Written Archives Centre, Caversham (BBC WAC in the following). Excerpts from BBC scripts and memoranda are included with the permission of the BBC Written Archives Centre, Caversham.

[2] 'Layout of BBC Broadcasts in German' (3 September 1940), E1/758/1, BBC WAC.

[3] 'Extract from Output Report of B.B.C. European Services dated January 10th-16th 1942' [corrected to 1943], E1/758/2, BBC WAC.

peaceful, ordinary Germans.[4] As a 1943 report stated: 'We have always made a distinction between the German war machine and the German people'.[5] The reports of the White Rose which filtered through to the BBC in April 1943 helped to strengthen this policy of distinguishing between Germans and Nazis.

Although news was the German Service's main business during wartime, no news bulletins survive in the archives, meaning that we can only trace the White Rose's appearance in other formats, including political commentary and features. Some recurring mistakes and omissions indicate that the BBC's information was somewhat limited: none of the scripts mention Alexander Schmorell or Willi Graf, and Sophie Scholl's name is given throughout as 'Sofia'. Moreover, none of the scripts refer to the group as the 'White Rose', since this name only came into common usage after 1945. Instead, the resistance movement is sometimes called the 'Scholl organisation'.

The first German Service programme to mention the White Rose members was a talk on 16 April 1943 by Austrian émigré Robert Lucas (born Robert Ehrenzweig, 1904–1984) entitled 'The Students Awake':

> In February, students of Munich University distributed leaflets in front of the main university building, in which the National Socialist regime was attacked in the

---

[4] See Stephanie Seul, '"Plain, unvarnished news"? The BBC German Service and Chamberlain's Propaganda Campaign Directed at Nazi Germany, 1938-1940', *Media History* 21 (2015), 378–96 (p. 385).
[5] 'Extract from Output Report of B.B.C. European Services dated January 10th-16th 1942' [corrected to 1943], E1/758/2, BBC WAC.

strongest terms, with Hitler being called a 'murderer'.
Many arrests were made. Several students were executed.
The names of three of the executed students are known:
Hans Scholl, a medical student, 24 years old, his sister
Sofia Scholl, 21 years old, and Christoph Probst, also a
medical student, 23 years old. According to a report
which has reached us from abroad, […] when Hans
Scholl was sentenced to death, he said to the judges: 'Soon
you will stand where I now stand.' […] After the
executions had been carried out, friends of the freedom
fighters wrote the following words in large black letters
on the university walls: […] We honour the memory of
the German students who have sacrificed their lives in the
fight for Germany's freedom.[6]

Lucas presents the actions of the White Rose as indicating
widespread unrest among German students, claiming that they are
beginning to remember the role played historically by student

---

[6] 'Im Februar verteilten Studenten der Universität München vor dem
Universitätsgebäude Flugblätter, in denen das nationalsozialistische Regime
auf das heftigste angegriffen und Hitler 'Mörder' genannt wurde. Es wurden
viele Verhaftungen vorgenommen. Mehrere Studenten wurden
hingerichtet. Die Namen von drei hingerichteten Studenten sind bekannt:
Hans Scholl, Student der Medizin, 24 Jahre alt, seine Schwester Sofia Scholl,
21 Jahre alt, und Christoph Probst, ebenfalls Student der Medizin 23 Jahre
alt. In einem Bericht, der aus dem Ausland gedrungen ist, heißt es: […] Als
Hans Scholl zum Tode verurteilt wurde, sagte er zu den Richtern: 'Bald
werdet Ihr stehen, wo ich jetzt stehe.' […] Nachdem die Hinrichtungen
vollzogen waren, schrieben Freunde der Freiheitskämpfer in großen
schwarzen Lettern diese Worte auf die Mauern der Universität: […] Wir
ehren das Andenken der deutschen Studenten, die im Kampf für die Freiheit
Deutschlands ihr Leben geopfert haben.' Robert Ehrenzweig, 'The Students
Awake' (16 April 1943), German Service Scripts: Features (January–June
1943), BBC WAC.

movements in Germany's struggle for freedom. This leads him to overestimate the White Rose's contemporary influence among German students:

> Songs and poems from the Wars of Liberation (1812/13) and from the days of the liberal 1848 revolution are being passed from hand to hand at the universities: impassioned calls by Ernst Moritz Arndt and Theodor Koerner for a holy war against the tyrant.[7]

The script ends on a hopeful, almost triumphal note, with music and the recitation of Ludwig August Frankl's 1848 poem 'Die Universität', which hails universities as cradles of liberal thought.

Ten days later, the German Service again presented the White Rose as proof of a wider student uprising in a feature by British actor Marius Goring (1912–1998), who worked as the German Service's Head of Features throughout the war.[8] The script revolves around the German song 'Freiheit, die ich meine' (1815–1818). Despite its origins in the liberal student movements of the early nineteenth century, by 1932 the song had been co-opted by the Nazis, appearing in several collections of national-socialist and SA songs. Goring adds a personal connection to his feature by recalling the first time he heard the song in 1931 as a student at Munich University, which he praises for its commitment to freedom of

---

[7] 'Lieder und Gedichte aus den Freiheitskriegen 1812/13 und aus den Tagen der freiheitlichen Revolution 1848 wandern jetzt in den Hochschulen von Hand zu Hand. Flammende Aufrufe von Ernst Moritz Arndt, Theodor Koerner, die zum heiligen Krieg gegen den Tyrannen auffordern.' Ibid.
[8] On the air Goring always appeared under the pseudonym Charles Richardson, presumably wishing to avoid any confusion between his surname and Reichsmarshall Goering.

thought at that time. The script chronicles the rise of Nazism among Goring's fellow students, before introducing the key news item: the execution of Hans Scholl, Sophie Scholl, and Christoph Probst. Goring characterises his own fellow students of 1931 as 'a doomed generation, [...] which was completely poisoned by Nazi teachings' ('einer untergehenden Generation, [...] die von den Nazi Lehren vollkommen vergiftet war'), but expresses the hope that this new generation of Munich students has 'a different worldview' ('ein anderes Weltbild').[9] As in the previous script, Hans Scholl's response to the judge who sentenced him is quoted, followed immediately by a verse from the song:

> Where men can be found
> Who for honour and justice
> Bravely will unite,
> There dwells a free race.[10]

By reminding his listeners of a former, better Germany before the days of Hitler, Goring reclaims the original meaning of the song about freedom. This emotive appeal to a shared sense of free 'Germanness' re-contextualises a familiar folk song to show that the members of the White Rose died for their commitment to values which predated the rise of Nazism and should be shared by all Germans.

---

[9] 'Wo sich Männer finden, / Die für Ehr und Recht / Mutig sich verbinden, / Weilt ein frei Geschlecht.' Marius Goring, 'Freiheit die ich meine' (25 April 1943), German Service Scripts: Features (January–June 1943), BBC WAC.
[10] Ibid.

In addition to linking the White Rose to a historical tradition within Germany, the BBC also attempted to present it as embodying pan-European resistance against Hitler. A script for the German women's programme claims that 'the young men and women of the Scholl organisation are [...] part of the movement of young people throughout Europe who are building the Europe of the future, the Europe which will arise when the Hitler regime has been smashed'.[11] Listing instances from Czechoslovakia, France, the Netherlands, and Greece, the script places the two Scholl siblings within a wider context of student resistance to the Third Reich. It also uses the Munich students as proof that their generation is not entirely united in support for Hitler:

> The youth of Germany seemed a generation pathetic but also dangerous in its ignorance. Now we know it is otherwise. There are at least some sections of the German youth brought up entirely under Nazism who have yet seen the worthlessness of the Nazi system.[12]

Looking ahead to a post-war future, the script claims that 'the knowledge that the Scholl Organisation existed and perhaps still exists brings relief to all those who have the future well-being of Europe at heart'.[13] By presenting the White Rose as proof 'that there is a section of the youth of Germany who will be able to co-operate with the United Nations in the reconstruction of Europe after the war', this script suggests that German young people are not

---

[11] Maurice B. Latey, 'German Women's Programme: Students Unite' (1 May 1943), German Service: Sonderbericht Scripts (January 1943 – April 1945), BBC WAC.
[12] Ibid.
[13] Ibid.

irredeemably lost to the cause of Nazism, but can choose to stand up to the regime and unite with fellow students across national borders.

Several other scripts presented the White Rose as indicative of a more widespread change in attitude among the German population. Under the programmatic title 'Fiat Justitia', a broadcast by Robert Lucas on 24 April 1943 focused on the decision a year earlier to appoint Hitler head of the German justice system. The White Rose members are listed among the many ordinary German victims of arbitrary Nazi justice. The feature details the fate of Germans whose businesses have been closed by the government, and those who have been sentenced to death for their political convictions, ending with the example of the Munich students. Once again quoting Hans Scholl's response to the judges sentencing him ('Soon you will stand where I now stand'), the script concludes: 'His words will come true, because the men who have destroyed justice in Germany will soon have to face the full force of the law themselves'.[14]

The sense of a growing internal opposition movement was emphasised in a commentary by Hungarian-born director and dramatist Martin Esslin (born Julius Pereszlenyi, 1918–2002), entitled 'The Objective Opposition' and delivered by Hugh Carleton Greene on 7 June 1943. The talk opens with a recent statement by Goebbels, criticising people who question official propaganda: 'today we have no sympathy for objectivity: we regard it as a danger and a threat to

---

[14] 'Sein Wort wird in Erfüllung gehen, denn die Gerechtigkeit wird vollzogen werden an den Männern, die das Recht in Deutschland zerstört haben.' Robert Ehrenzweig, 'Fiat Justitia' (24 April 1943), German Service Scripts: Features (January–June 1943), BBC WAC.

our national interests'.[15] Greene debunks Goebbels's claim that the
proportion of these kinds of Germans is insignificant by giving
examples from many different sections of German society who have
spoken out against the Nazis. His examples include Church leaders,
prominent judges, workers sentenced to death for belonging to the
Communist Party, a mother who wrote an open letter criticising the
state's use of children as cannon-fodder, and the German soldiers
who surrendered to the Allies at Tunisia. By judging their situation
objectively, the script maintains, all of these people have reached the
conclusion that they cannot support the Nazi regime. The final
example of 'objective' people is that of the White Rose members. The
script quotes a long passage from leaflet VI, accusing the Hitler
regime of perverting the meaning of the words 'freedom' and
'honour' and calling on the German youth to salvage Germany's
reputation by rising up against the Nazis. This builds towards the
talk's conclusion:

> As you can see, [...] the number of Germans who have
> preserved or rediscovered clear thinking is not as small as
> Goebbels would have it. All the groups of which I have
> spoken have rejected the Hitler regime. They have
> rejected it, because within the sphere in which they came
> into contact with it — religion, law, work, the family,
> military reality, the intellectual life of the university —
> [...] they recognised the regime's hypocrisy. All of these
> people lack only one thing: the knowledge that there are

---

[15] '[...] für Objektivität haben <u>wir</u> heute kein Verständnis. Wir halten sie
für eine Gefahr und eine Bedrohung unserer nationalen Interessen.' Julius
Pereszlenyi, 'The Objective Opposition' (7 June 1943), German Service
Scripts: Features (January–June 1943), BBC WAC.

other Germans who think exactly as they do; the knowledge that they are not alone.[16]

By broadcasting excerpts from one of the White Rose's leaflets and situating it within the context of widespread opposition, the BBC tried to broaden its appeal beyond the university and assure clandestine listeners that they were part of a larger movement gathering momentum within Germany.

The final broadcast on the White Rose came from the German Service's most famous contributor, Thomas Mann, on 27 June 1943. From 1940 onwards Mann, the only German national allowed to voice his own opinions on the air, had contributed monthly commentaries, which always began with a direct address to 'German listeners!' ('Deutsche Hörer!').[17] Echoing the language of freedom and honour in the fourth pamphlet, Mann uses the example of the White Rose activists to make explicit the distinction between Germans and Nazis:

> I say: honour to the people of Europe! And I add something which may sound strange to some listeners:

---

[16] 'Sie sehen: [...] die Zahl der Deutschen, die sich ihr klares Denken bewährt oder wiedergefunden haben ist nicht so klein, wie Goebbels es haben will. Alle die Gruppen von Menschen von denen ich gesprochen habe, haben das Hitler-Regime abgelehnt. Sie haben es abgelehnt, weil sie in der Sphäre in der sie mit ihm in Berührung gekommen waren: der Religion, dem Recht, der Arbeit, der Familie, der militärischen Wirklichkeit, dem geistigen Leben der Universität – [...] die Verlogenheit des Regimes erkannt hatten. All diesen Menschen fehlt nur eines: Das Wissen davon, dass es noch andere Deutsche gibt, die genau so denken, die Erkenntnis, dass sie nicht allein sind.' Ibid.

[17] See Thomas Mann, *Deutsche Hörer! 55 Radiosendungen nach Deutschland von Thomas Mann* (Stockholm: Bermann-Fischer Verlag, 1945), p. 11.

honour and sympathy also to the German people! The
lesson that one may not distinguish between the German
people and the Nazis [...] is frequently upheld — not
without intelligence — in the Allied countries. But it is
untenable and will not persist. Too many facts speak
against it.[18]

Despite a number of factual errors (Hans Scholl is called a 'survivor
of Stalingrad', and Probst's first name is given as 'Adrian'), Mann
gives an impassioned account of the White Rose's bravery, claiming
that its members died 'a martyr's death' ('Märtyrertod') and that their
words have restored the reputation of the German youth.[19] He ends
with a direct address to the White Rose members:

Upstanding, wonderful young people! You shall not have
died in vain; you shall not be forgotten. The Nazis have
erected memorials to dirty rowdies, to base killers in
Germany — but the true German revolution will tear
them down and in their place memorialise your names.
You, who when Germany and Europe were still
shrouded in night, knew and proclaimed: 'A new faith in
freedom and honour is dawning.'[20]

---

[18] 'Ich sage: Ehre den Völkern Europas! Und ich füge etwas hinzu, was im
Augenblick manchem, der mich hört, befremdlich klingen mag: Ehre und
Mitgefühl auch dem deutschen Volk! Die Lehre, daß man zwischen ihm
und dem Nazitum nicht unterscheiden dürfe, [...] wird in den Ländern der
Alliierten zuweilen, nicht ohne Geist, vertreten; aber sie ist unhaltbar und
wird sich nicht durchsetzen. Zuviele Tatsachen sprechen dagegen.'. Ibid.,
p. 93.
[19] Ibid., p. 94.
[20] 'Brave, herrliche junge Leute! Ihr sollt nicht umsonst gestorben, sollt nicht
vergessen sein. Die Nazis haben schmutzigen Rowdies, gemeinen Killern
in Deutschland Denkmäler gesetzt — die deutsche Revolution, die

In a fitting echo to Sophie Scholl's scattering of leaflets in the Munich University atrium, Mann's verbal memorial to the Munich group was subsequently printed on leaflets and dropped over Germany by the RAF between 3 December 1943 and 16 March 1944, thus spreading its message even further.[21]

Once the war was over, the BBC German Service received thousands of letters from Germany every month, detailing just how important its broadcasts had been to listeners during the darkest days of Nazi rule. In July 1946, 'a young listener in Nürnberg, Dieter Sasse, the half brother of the executed Munich student Christoph Probst', wrote to the BBC 'a full account of the Munich Students' revolt in 1943'.[22] This was deemed 'an interesting document of some historical importance', as well as 'a very moving personal account by an idealistic young man of the anti-Nazi movement'.[23] Although Sasse's account was to be broadcast in full, sadly, no record of the script survives in the archives.

What, then, can the surviving BBC broadcasts on the White Rose tell us about its influence inside and outside Germany? Just as the defeat at Stalingrad marked a turning point in Germans' perception of the war, news of a resistance group within the heart of

---

wirkliche, wird sie niederreißen und an ihrer Stelle eure Namen verewigen, die ihr, als noch Nacht über Deutschland und Europa lag, wußtet und verkündetet: "Es dämmert ein neuer Glaube an Freiheit und Ehre."' Ibid.

[21] See Sonja Valentin, *'Steine in Hitlers Fenster': Thomas Manns Radiosendungen 'Deutsche Hörer!' (1940–1945)* (Göttingen: Wallstein Verlag, 2015), p. 204.

[22] Christina Gibson, 'Evidence on the German Audience for British Broadcasts' (6 July 1946), p. 8, E3/275/1, BBC WAC.

[23] Ibid.

the 'Third Reich' was perceived by international news media as an important indicator of internal opposition to Hitler's regime. The BBC German Service seized upon this narrative, because it tied in perfectly within its policy of distinguishing between ordinary Germans and Nazis, and presented an opportunity for appealing to the good in every German listener. The news of the White Rose enabled the German Service to fulfil its claims to truth by reporting factual information on the group's activism and their oppression by the state, while the messages contained within their leaflets and statements in court could also be crafted into a valuable strand of 'hope propaganda' encouraging more widespread opposition to Hitler across national and social divides.

Emily Oliver is a Leverhulme Early Career Fellow at the University of Warwick leading the research project 'Broadcasting Nations: A History of the BBC German Service (1938-1999)'. Her research focuses on Anglo-German cultural relations in the twentieth century. After gaining a PhD at the University of Birmingham, she worked as Postdoctoral Research Associate at King's College London on the European Research Council project 'Beyond Enemy Lines: Literature and Film in the British and American Zones of Occupied Germany'. Her monograph, 'Shakespeare and German Reunification' is published by Peter Lang (2017).

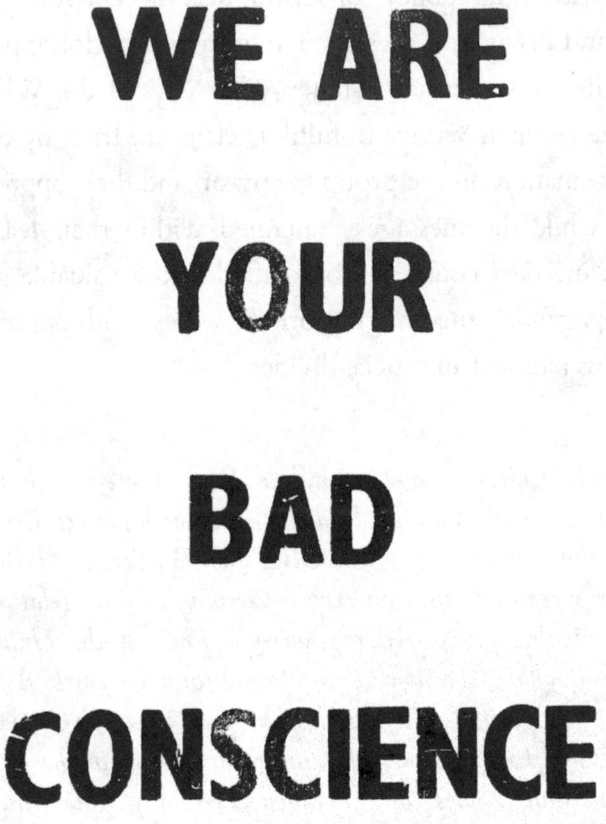

WE ARE

YOUR

BAD

CONSCIENCE

Figure 3. Poster designed and printed by student translators at the Bodleian's Bibliographical Press.

'WE ARE YOUR BAD CONSCIENCE': THE WHITE ROSE AND RESISTANCE TO UNJUST LAW

Paul Yowell

The leaflets that the White Rose students distributed in 1942–43 were a call to resistance against the Nazi regime. They called for various acts of non-violent sabotage and looked forward to the overthrow of Hitler, but above all they attempted to persuade Germans of their moral duty to resist the Third Reich in their minds and hearts. 'We will not be silent', the fourth leaflet proclaimed. 'We are your bad conscience. The White Rose will never leave in you in peace.' They wanted to trouble the minds of a German people that had, step by step, with increasing complacency, come to accept Hitler as the *Führer* and to avert their eyes from the atrocities being carried out around them.

Hans and Sophie Scholl were executed for their role in distributing the leaflets, along with Christoph Probst, on 22 February 1943, followed by several others connected to the White Rose later in the year. The reasoning that led them to resist, to protest, and to risk their lives, is revealed in letters, diaries, and other sources, including transcripts of their interrogation at the hands of the Gestapo. The interrogation of Sophie is the centrepiece in Marc Rothemund's 2005 film *Sophie Scholl — The Final Days (Sophie Scholl — Die letzten Tage)*, where the fate of the White Rose is seen through her eyes. In the film she is in some ways a composite figure,[1] reflecting several common themes in the thought and ideas of various members of the group. While she was not involved in writing the White Rose leaflets, she was intellectually and spiritually in tune those who did, especially with Hans.[2] This essay will use the film's interrogation scene to illustrate themes regarding conscience and unjust laws, connecting the dialogue to historical records and to philosophical literature.

After their arrest at the Ludwig Maximilian University for passing out leaflets there, in February of 1943, Hans and Sophie initially denied their involvement. But investigators soon obtained enough evidence to force their confessions, and Sophie's interrogation then moves from the details of the operation to the motivations and reasons behind it. She is questioned by Robert Mohr, a former police officer who had become a Gestapo agent. At the beginning of one scene, after giving her a cup of coffee, he explains why Sophie and the White Rose students are facing punishment and meets a spirited response:

> Mohr: Because that's what the law requires. Without law there is no order.

> Sophie: The law you're referring to protected free speech before the Nazis came to power in 1933. Someone who speaks freely now is imprisoned or put to death. What does this have to do with order?

---

[1] See Elizabeth M. Ward's essay in the present volume, pp. 79–95.
[2] See Paul Shrimpton, *Conscience before Conformity: Hans and Sophie Scholl and the White Rose Resistance in Nazi Germany* (Leominster: Gracewing, 2017).

Mohr: What can we rely on if not the law — no matter who wrote it?

Sophie: On our conscience.

Mohr: Nonsense! Here is the law [lifting a legal code from his desk]. And here are the people [lifting another book]. As a criminal investigator, it is my duty to find out if they are consistent [moving the first book onto the second], and if not, where the rotten spot is.

Sophie: The law changes. Conscience doesn't.

Mohr: What would happen if everyone decided on his own what is right or wrong?[3]

These words represent screenwriter Fred Breinersdorfer's imaginative but historically based reconstruction of Mohr's interrogation of Sophie. A strength of the film's screenplay is that it is carefully grounded in the documentary records, including interrogation transcripts, the White Rose leaflets, and other sources. Another strength of the film is that Mohr is not drawn as a simple caricature of a Nazi antagonist. Beneath the surface of aggressive interrogation, he seems to have a deep respect for Sophie. He tries to persuade her to renounce her rebellion against Hitler's government, which he believes has advanced the good of the German people. If she recants, he implies that she will survive, with a lighter

---

[3] For quotations of the interrogation scene in this chapter, I rely mainly on the subtitles of the English-language DVD of *Sophie Scholl*, but have introduced some minor changes that, in my view, reflect more closely the German original script.

punishment. But when it becomes apparent that she will not be persuaded, he threatens death.

The official transcript from the Gestapo files states at the end:

> Final Question: During this entire interrogation, which has stretched over two full days, we have discussed various political and philosophical questions, [this transcript] touching only the high points. After these exchanges, have you not come to the conclusion that your conduct — and the concerted action you, your brother, and others undertook — must be viewed as a crime against the common good, as well as and especially against our troops who are fighting long and hard in the east? Especially in this phase of the war? And that this conduct and action must be met with the most severe sentence possible?

> Answer: From my point of view, I must answer no. Now as before, I believe I have done the best that I could for my nation. I therefore do not regret my conduct. I wish to take upon myself the consequences of my actions.[4]

The discussion of political and philosophical questions referenced here is what screenwriter Breinersdorfer aims to reconstruct, in the dialogue about law above and as they turn to debate Germany's predicament.

---

[4] Third Interrogation of Sophie Scholl, 20 Febrauary 1943, at <https://whiterosehistory.com/1943/02/20/sophie-scholl-third-interrogation/> [accessed 14 May 2019].

Mohr: You're so gifted. Why don't you think and feel like us? Freedom, honor, prosperity, a morally responsible government. That is our conviction.

Scholl: Weren't your eyes opened by the terrible bloodbath that Nazis carried out in all of Europe, in the name of freedom and honor? Germany will be disgraced forever if its youth doesn't topple Hitler and build a new intellectual Europe.

Mohr: The new Europe can only be National Socialist.

Scholl: What if your Führer is insane?

Mohr: Our German soldiers are fighting for a free Germany. Never again will Germany be occupied, that I tell you.

Scholl: Until the world is over, and foreign troops come marching in, and everyone in the world points its finger at us for tolerating Hitler.

Describing his method in an interview, Breinersdorfer said that he took 'no more than ten' sentences directly from the transcripts, which were a 'summary' rather than a literal transcription, and yet provide a clear picture of what happened during the four days in the Gestapo prison. 'I also developed a lot of dialogue from the White Rose leaflets', he said, 'so the script is a mixture. The main thing is the documents allowed us to reconstruct exactly what happened.'[5] Among the sources are statements by Sophie's cellmate during her interrogation, Else Gebel, and Mohr's son, Willi; and a

---

[5] Richard Phillips, 'Fred Breinersdorfer, writer of Sophie Scholl — The Final Days, speaks with the WSWS' <www.wsws.org/en/articles/2006/08/soph-a17.html> [accessed 9 May 2019].

memorandum by Mohr himself, which is somewhat unreliable due its self-serving nature but of historical value.

Frank McDonough, an historian of the Third Reich, writes that Mohr treated Sophie like an errant daughter and that 'Willi recalls ... that whenever his father spoke to him in confidence about the case of Sophie Scholl, he said he was impressed by her and treated her well.'[6] Sophie told Gebel that the long second interrogation by Mohr was 'exhausting but interesting', as he had apparently chosen to play 'good cop' in dealing with an intelligent and well-spoken university student, even giving her a cup of good coffee.[7] During the third and final interrogation, as Gebel relates Sophie's story, Mohr lectured her on National Socialism and loyalty to the Führer and German armed forces, to which Sophie responded by saying, 'I would do exactly the same thing again. It is you who has a mistaken worldview'.[8] Mohr claimed that he 'tried to use my powers of persuasion to get Miss Scholl to say she did not agree with her brother's ideology' and to admit she had been only an assistant.[9] Had she done this, Mohr said, she would have been spared; instead she chose to stand with Hans and die for her principles.[10]

Breinersdorfer's portrayal of Mohr and his discussion with Sophie gains further credence when read in light of legal philosopher Gustav Radbruch. Already well known in Germany before World War II, Radbruch gained international recognition through post-

---

[6] Frank McDonough, *Sophie Scholl: The Real Story of the Woman Who Defied Hitler* (Stroud: The History Press, 2009), p. 128.
[7] Ibid., p. 132.
[8] Ibid., p. 136.
[9] Ibid.
[10] Ibid.

war writings arguing that there are moral limits on what can count as valid law. In one essay, he describes a legal profession that had come to accept an absolute duty to obey whatever has been laid down as a positive law, an idea that had been successfully taught to the German people:

> 'An order is an order', the soldier is told. 'A law is a law', says the jurist. The soldier, however, is required neither by duty nor by law to obey an order whose object he knows to be a felony or a misdemeanor, while the jurist — since the last of the natural lawyers died out a hundred years ago — recognizes no such exceptions to the validity of a law or to the requirement of obedience by those subject to it. A law is valid because it is a law, and it is a law if, in the general run of cases, it has the power to prevail.
>
> This view of a law and of its validity (we call it the positivistic theory) has rendered jurists and the people alike defenceless against arbitrary, cruel, or criminal laws, however extreme they might be. In the end, the positivistic theory equates law with power; there is law only where there is power.[11]

In referring to 'natural lawyers', Radbruch had in mind the tradition that runs through Plato, Aristotle, and Augustine and reaches a high point with Aquinas, who taught that laws that are contrary to human good do not bind in conscience, and are like acts of violence rather than law.[12] Records indicate that at one meeting of the Scholls and

---

[11] Gustav Radbruch, 'Five Minutes of Legal Philosophy (1945)', trans. by Bonnie Litschewski Paulson and Stanley L. Paulson, *Oxford Journal of Legal Studies* 26 (2006), 13-15 (p. 13).
[12] S.T. I-II q 96 art 4.

their friends in the summer of 1941, they discussed Aquinas on systems of government and on legitimate forms of rebellion.[13] The third White Rose leaflet, which cites Augustine and Aristotle, shows the students' acquaintance with the natural law tradition and contemporary interpreters of it such as Etienne Gilson.[14] The leaflet states:

> [E]very single person is entitled to a viable and just government that ensures the freedom of the individual as well as the welfare of society as a whole. For each person should, in accordance with God's will, freely and independently seek to achieve their natural goal, that is their earthly happiness through self-reliance and initiative, while co-existing and co-operating within the state as a community.

The present German state, however, is a 'dictatorship of evil'; the fourth leaflet calls it an 'Un-State' ('Unstaat').

The 'positivistic' theory that Radbruch contrasts with natural law theory embraces not only a view of what counts as law,[15] but the proposition that there is an absolute duty to obey the law — a duty binding not only on judges and members of the legal profession but

---

[13] *At the Heart of the White Rose: Letters and Diaries of Hans and Sophie Scholl*, ed. by Inge Jens (New York: Harper & Row, 1987), p. 161.

[14] See Paul Shrimpton's essay in this volume, noting Hans's reading of Gilson's *Introduction à l'étude de Saint Augustin* (1929).

[15] What Radbruch calls the positivistic theory needs to be distinguished from the positivism that was adopted by legal philosophers in the post-war period. In the English-speaking tradition that has followed H.L.A. Hart, positivism is a theory concerned with identifying what counts as law — the criteria of legal validity — but it is not directly concerned with or premised upon any particular view of the obligations of people to obey the law or of judges to apply it.

also on ordinary citizens, and which requires them to accept anything laid down in a statute as valid law. Mohr, as portrayed in the film, is in the grip of such a theory, seen in his cold dismissal of Sophie's appeal to conscience and his rigorous insistence on the contents of the law-book.

It is easy for us to side with Sophie in the interrogation dialogue, from our twenty-first-century perspective. The twentieth century was not only darkened by the Nazi regime and WWII, but filled with the cruelty of other totalitarian movements, as well as colonial and other regimes that sponsored oppressive discrimination. We look back and admire those who resisted: Solzhenitsyn and other Russian dissidents, Gandhi, Martin Luther King Jr, and many others. It is easy to forget that leading figures in political philosophy in the centuries that preceded WWII provided little encouragement for conscience-based acts of resistance. Rather they provided succour for the likes of Mohr and the millions of individuals who likewise acquiesced in oppression and tyranny.

From the early modern period forward, many philosophers taught that obedience to the law should be absolute or nearly so. Immanuel Kant thought that if a ruler acts against the law, 'subjects may indeed oppose this injustice by complaints but not by resistance'.[16] In *Practical Philosophy* he asks, 'Is rebellion a legitimate means for a people to throw off the oppressive power of a so-called tyrant?' The answer: '[I]t is still in the highest degree wrong of the subjects to seek their right in this way, and they cannot in the least complain about injustice if, having failed in this conflict, they have

---

[16] Kant, *The Metaphysics of Morals*, trans. and ed. by Mary Gregor (Cambridge: Cambridge University Press, 1996).

to suffer the most severe punishment.'[17] David Hume advocated 'exact' obedience to the law, with reasoning that Mohr would have found congenial: 'A small degree of experience and observation suffices to teach us, that society cannot possibly be maintained without the authority of magistrates, and that this authority must soon fall into contempt, where exact obedience is not paid to it.'[18] Some social contract theorists, notably Locke, argued that when rulers violate natural rights, the people are released from the contract and may rebel. But others in this tradition, including Hobbes, argued that the contract is unbreakable, and that the absolute authority of the state is necessary to prevent a descent back into the chaos of the state of nature. Utilitarianism is sometimes thought to provide more leeway to individuals, allowing them to choose to violate the law if, in their judgment, this is for the greater good. But Jeremy Bentham, probably the most influential utilitarian, allowed for disobedience to the law only as part of large-scale group effort to overthrow the current regime, which must be based on a careful calculation both that the effort will produce greater overall utility and that it is likely to succeed.[19] He said, like Kant, that the individual can criticise injustice but must submit to the law; the motto of the good citizen is '[t]o obey punctually; to censure freely'.[20] He railed against those who appeal to conscience or principles of natural law to justify a

---

[17] Kant, *Practical Philosophy,* trans. and ed. by Mary Gregor (Cambridge: Cambridge University Press, 1997).

[18] David Hume, 'Of the Original Contract', cited in *The Cambridge Companion to Hume*, ed. by David Norton (Cambridge: Cambridge University Press, 1993), p. 5.

[19] Jeremy Bentham, *A Fragment on Government* (Union, NJ: The Lawbook Exchange, 2001), p. 101.

[20] Ibid.

personal decision to disobey the law. He famously derided the notion of natural rights as nonsense, stating, 'There are no rights without law — no rights contrary to the law — no rights anterior to the law.'[21] And he mocked the notion of an individuated 'right to resist oppression'.[22]

So Mohr, in his strict fealty to the law over personal conscience, was in the company of renowned philosophers. Moreover, by Radbruch's estimation in the quotation above, the last adherents of natural law theory had died out in Germany a century before. The experience of WWII led Radbruch, like many others, to rethink their views of legal authority. In 1946 Radbruch wrote:

> There are principles of law, therefore, that are weightier than any legal enactment, so that a law in conflict with them is devoid of validity. These principles are known as natural law or the law of reason.[23]

There are hints of such a view in his pre-war work, but it is only after the war that he proclaims it clearly. In his 1932 treatise on legal philosophy, Radbruch argued that citizens were morally free to follow their conscience and violate unjust laws.[24] For judges,

---

[21] Jeremy Bentham, 'Anarchical Fallacies', in *The Works of Jeremy Bentham*, vol. 3, ed. by John Bowring (Edinburgh: William Tait, 1838-1843), p. 221.
[22] Ibid, vol. 2, p. 504. Bentham said that such a right leads to an anarchical attitude that prescribes as follows 'Submit not to any decree or other act of power, of the justice of which you are not yourself perfectly convinced. If a constable call upon you to serve in the militia, shoot the constable and not the enemy. … If a judge sentences you to be imprisoned or put to death, have a dagger ready, and take a stroke first at the judge'. Ibid.
[23] Radbruch, 'Five Minutes of Legal Philosophy', p. 14.
[24] Radbruch, *Rechtsphilosophie* (Heidelberg: CF Müller Verlag, 2003).

however, he considered their professional obligation to the law to be paramount. Judges cannot elevate their conscience over the law even where it threatens to work injustice. He noted that while we condemn as a hypocrite the parson who preaches doctrine contrary to his personal conviction, we respect the judge who gives judgment according to the law even when that conflicts with his personal sense of fairness.[25]

Following the war, Radbruch maintained this view of a judge's legal obligation, but he argued that statutes that reach an extreme degree of injustice are not valid laws but merely purported laws.[26] The logical move here is similar to saying that a prescription written by a doctor with murderous intent is a *recipe for poison* rather than a *true prescription*. With regard to laws that involve only a moderate degree of injustice, either in their content or the way they are applied in a given case, Radbruch thought that judges had a duty to apply them as valid laws. Acknowledging the difficulty of distinguishing between moderate and extreme justice, Radbruch argued that we can find one dividing line in the principle of human equality:

> Where there is not even an attempt at justice, where equality, the core of justice, is deliberately betrayed in the issuance of positive law, then the statute is not merely 'flawed law', it lacks completely the very nature of law. For law, including positive law, cannot be otherwise

[25] Ibid.

[26] Gustav Radbruch, 'Statutory Lawlessness and Supra-Statutory Law (1946)', trans. by Bonnie Litschewski Paulson and Stanley L. Paulson, *Oxford Journal of Legal Studies* 26 (2006), 1–11 (p. 7). While some scholars argue that Radbruch underwent a conversion, he maintained that he was bringing out into the open what was hidden in the shadows in his pre–war work.

defined than as a system and an institution whose very meaning is to serve justice. Measured by this standard, whole portions of National Socialist law never attained the dignity of valid law.[27]

The reason for this conclusion about Nazi law is that its 'explicit intention from the very beginning [was to] extricate itself from the essential requirement of justice, namely, the equal treatment of equals'. And, Radbruch argued, '[l]egal character is also lacking in all the statutes that treated human beings as subhuman and denied them human rights'.[28]

Sophie is alert to this dimension of the relationship between law and morality, and the importance of human equality, in the following segment of Breinersdorfer's screenplay, where she pushes back against Mohr's defence of the Nazi government.

> Sophie: Take racial hatred. We had a Jewish teacher in Ulm. He was placed before a group of SA men. They had to spit in his face. That night he disappeared, like thousands in Munich. Allegedly to work in Eastern Europe.
>
> Mohr: You believe that nonsense? The Jews were emigrating, of their own choice.
>
> Sophie: Soldiers coming from the East talk of extermination camps. Hitler wants to exterminate all European Jews! He was preaching that madness 20 years

---

[27] Ibid.
[28] Ibid., p. 8.

ago. How can you believe that the Jews are different than we are?

Mohr: That mob brought us misfortune, but you are confused. You have no idea. The wrong education. Maybe it's our fault. I'd have raised a girl like you differently.

Sophie: Do you realise how shocked I was to find out that the Nazis used gas and poison to dispose of mentally ill children? My mother's friends told us. Trucks came to pick up the children at the mental hospital. The other children asked where they were going. 'They're going to heaven', said the nurses. So the children got on the truck singing. You think I wasn't raised right because I feel pity for them?

Mohr: These are lives not worth living. You have had training as a children's nurse. You saw people who were mentally ill.

Sophie: Yes, and that's why I know. No one, regardless of circumstances, can pass divine judgment. No one knows what goes on in the minds of the mentally ill. No one knows how much wisdom can come from suffering. Every life is precious.

Mohr: You have to realise that a new age has dawned. What you're saying has nothing to do with reality.

Sophie: Of course it has to do with reality. With decency, morals, and God.

Mohr: God! There is no God.

One wonders whether, at some point in the course of becoming a member of the National Socialist party and then a Gestapo agent, Mohr felt pangs of conscience. Perhaps he had some sense of common humanity that initially recoiled at the term the Nazi party used to push its ideology that some lives are not worth living: 'lebensunwertes Leben'. If so, Mohr eventually succumbed to the Nazi regime's effort to suppress conscience. That effort was overt and led by Hitler himself, who said: 'Conscience is a Jewish invention. It is a [mutilation], like circumcision. [...] There is no truth, either in the moral or in the scientific sense.'[29] Hermann Göring said starkly, 'I have no conscience. My conscience is Adolf Hitler.'[30] As Hannah Arendt observed, Hitler would come to embody 'the law of the land', not simply for 'monsters, or raving sadists', but 'the most respected members of respectable society'.[31]

Mohr's scepticism about concentration camps and claim that the Jews are emigrating reflected a common German attitude. Even Albert Speer, Hitler's architect and minister for armaments and war production, was able to maintain at the Nuremberg trials and afterwards, with some plausibility, that he did not know of the facts of the Holocaust. A kind of willing blindness was widespread. In Speer's case later archival research proved that he almost certainly did know of the Holocaust, but the doubt that had lingered over this

[29] See Bernard Schumacher, 'The Dictatorship of the Conscience', *Nova et Vetera* (English Edition) 15 (2017), 547–78 (p. 548 & n. 2).
[30] Ibid. & n.5.
[31] Hannah Arendt, 'Personal Responsibility under Dictatorship', in *Responsibility and Judgment* (New York: Schocken Books, 2003), pp. 17–48 (p. 43): 'for them, it was enough that everything happened according to the "will of the Führer", which was the law of the land, and in accordance with the "words of the Führer", which had the force of law.'

shows how far-reaching the denial had been.[32] The White Rose leaflets included some of the first public denunciations of the Holocaust while it was ongoing.

In depicting Sophie's awareness of the evil and her decision to resist as motivated by her belief in God, Breinersdorfer's script reflects a sentence in the transcript of Sophie's third interrogation, where she gives an account of conversations that were had among the White Rose students:

> We also discussed general questions, now and then interspersed with political, philosophical, or theological questions. I remember that once we thoroughly discussed the question as to whether the Christian and National Socialist ideologies could ever be reconciled. After a longer debate, we finally mutually agreed that the Christian person was more accountable to God than to the State.[33]

Paul Shrimpton has shown that the White Rose students drew inspiration from several Christian writers, and that Sophie in particular was drawn to John Henry Newman.[34] She gave a volume of his sermons to her fiancé, and their correspondence indicates that Newman made a deep impression on them, in particular the sermon 'The Testimony of Conscience'.

---

[32] See Gilbert King, 'The Candor and Lies of Nazi Officer Albert Speer', <www.smithsonianmag.com/history/the-candor-and-lies-of-nazi-officer-albert-speer-324737/> [accessed 14 May 2019].

[33] Third Interrogation of Sophie Scholl, 20 Febrauary 1943, <https://whiterosehistory.com/1943/02/20/sophie-scholl-third-interrogation/> [accessed 14 May 2019].

[34] See Shrimpton's essay in this volume, pp. 23–35.

Hans and Sophie were tried on 22 February 1943 by Roland Freisler, the notorious judge Hitler had appointed to head the 'People's Court', which had jurisdiction over high treason, acts that undermine the war effort, and other political crimes. The harsh and vindictive rhetoric he uses toward the Scholls in the film is, again, no caricature, but true to a character that he consciously cultivated and used for purposes of intimidation.[35] It was a show trial, and the verdict of execution was reached swiftly. We have no exact account of what the defendants said during the trial, but there is some support for the words with which Breinersdorfer has Sophie account for her actions:[36] 'Somebody, after all, had to make a start. What we wrote and said is also believed by many others. They just don't dare express themselves as we did'. And the thought expressed here is consistent with abundant evidence of the Scholls' brave willingness to follow their conscience.[37] Hans's last words were, 'Long live freedom!' ('Es lebe die Freiheit!')[38] and found in his cell, written by him in chalk, was a line from Goethe: 'Allen Gewalten zum Trutz' — 'Stand firm against the powers that be'.

Dr Paul Yowell is Fellow and Tutor in Law at Oriel College and Associate Professor in the Law Faculty, University of Oxford. He teaches and researches in the fields of legal theory and public law, with particular interests in constitutional theory, comparative constitutional law, and human rights. He is the author of 'Constitutional Rights and Constitutional Design: Moral and

---

[35] McDonough, *Sophie Scholl*, pp. 140–42.
[36] Ibid., p. 143.
[37] See Shrimpton, *Conscience before Conformity*.
[38] McDonough, *Sophie Scholl*, p. 151.

Empirical Reasoning in Judicial Review' (2018) and co-author of 'Legislated Rights: Securing Human Rights Through Legislation' (2018).

MARC ROTHEMUND'S
SOPHIE SCHOLL —
DIE LETZTEN TAGE (2005)

Elizabeth M. Ward

On first viewing, it could be argued that Marc Rothemund's 2005 film, *Sophie Scholl — Die letzten Tage* (*Sophie Scholl — The Final Days*) breaks little new ground. Two feature films, Michael Verhoeven's *Die Weiße Rose* (*The White Rose*, 1982) and Percy Adlon's *Fünf letzte Tage* (*Five Last Days*, 1982), had already depicted the White Rose on screen, the latter of which had also focused on the final days of Sophie Scholl.[1] Rothemund's representational strategy in *Sophie Scholl — Die letzten Tage* is underpinned by the repeated use of a symbolism drawn from Christian martyrdom and by the foregrounding of Sophie's Christian faith, both of which were approaches often employed in West German cinema in which resisters were frequently cast both as 'victims of National Socialism and as prophets of the new democratic order'.[2]

---

[1] Lena Stolze played Sophie Scholl in both films. In 1983, Stolze was awarded the German Film Prize (then named the *Bundesfilmpreis*) for her roles in both films.

[2] David Clarke, 'German Martyrs: Images of Christianity and Resistance to National Socialism in German Cinema', in *Screening War: Perspectives on German Suffering*, ed. by Paul Cooke and Marc Silberman (Rochester, NY: Camden House, 2010), pp. 36–55 (pp. 36–37).

Of course, over two decades separate the films of Verhoeven and Adlon from Rothemund's *Sophie Scholl*. Yet even when placed within its contemporaneous production context, Rothemund's film was by no means an isolated example of a renewed interest in resistance in the Third Reich: Max Färberböck's *Aimée & Jaguar* (1999), Margarethe von Trotta's *Rosenstraße* (2003), Volker Schlöndorff's *Der neunte Tag* (*The Ninth Day*, 2004), Niko von Glasow's *Edelweißpiraten* (*Edelweiss Pirates*, 2004), and Jo Baier's *Stauffenberg* (2004) all deal with themes of resistance in German cinema.[3] Despite their different perspectives on the National Socialist past, these films are united by one core feature: they are made for audiences with no direct memory of, let alone involvement in, the events depicted. This historical estrangement called for a new approach in depicting the Third Reich, and it is striking how these films repeatedly draw upon universalising narratives above explicitly politicising forms of 'working through' the past (*Aufarbeitung der Vergangenheit*), as was the case in the Federal Republic and the German Democratic Republic. In doing so, they frequently depict how exceptional individuals in the Third Reich paved the way for a new, democratic order in post-war Germany. Rothemund's *Sophie Scholl* is no exception.

Sophie Scholl focuses on White Rose member, Sophie Scholl, from the eve of her arrest on 17 February 1943 to her execution on

---

[3] To these examples, we could add Costa-Gravas' *Amen* (2002), Oliver Hirschbiegel's *Der Untergang* (*Downfall*, 2004), Dennis Gansel's *Napola — Elite für den Führer* (*Before the Fall*, 2004), Lutz Hachmeister's *Das Goebbels-Experiment* (*The Goebbels Experiment*, 2005), Heinrich Breloer's *Speer und Er* (*Speer and Hitler: The Devil's Architect*, 2005), and Joseph Vilsmaier and Dana Vávrová's *Der letzte Zug* (*The Last Train*, 2006).

22 February 1943. The film opens with Sophie listening to the radio with her friend, Gisela, in Munich. Sophie then hastily leaves the house and we follow her through the streets of Munich before we see her enter a dark, unmarked building. Here she joins her brother, Hans, and other student members of the White Rose as they prepare to distribute their sixth pamphlet. The pamphlets are to be sent anonymously to addresses in Munich, but at the end of the evening the group realises that they have printed more than they can send. Hans decides to distribute the pamphlets anonymously at Munich's Ludwig Maximilian University the following morning. Sophie insists on helping him, and the next day they leave piles of pamphlets outside lecture halls and around the main university building. Fearful of detection, they hurriedly make to leave, when Sophie takes the spontaneous and fateful decision to push a pile of the pamphlets off the balcony. A caretaker spots them, and they are apprehended. The Gestapo is informed, and Sophie and Hans are arrested.

Here the film turns to its central focus: the interrogation of Sophie by the Gestapo officer, Robert Mohr. Over the course of four interviews, Sophie demonstrates why she is the 'bad conscience' ('böses Gewissen') of the National Socialist state: she refuses to counter Mohr's statements of party support with overtly political arguments, and instead repeatedly highlights the government's moral failures.[4] In the first interrogation, Sophie denies playing any role in the production of the pamphlets and insists she was merely playing a 'prank' when she pushed them off the balcony 'as is [her] nature' ('Solche Späße liegen in meiner Natur.'). When further evidence is

---

[4] This term was used in the concluding sentence of the group's fourth pamphlet.

found linking not only Sophie and Hans, but also the other group members, to the printing and distribution of the pamphlets, Sophie insists that she and Hans bear sole responsibility. At the end of her interrogation, Mohr offers Sophie the opportunity to save her life by denouncing Hans and Christoph Probst as the culprits. Sophie refuses. All three are charged with treason and are subjected to a show trial overseen by the notoriously harsh judge and president of the *Volksgerichtshof* (People's Court), Roland Freisler. They are pronounced guilty in a trial lasting less than an hour. Just four days after their arrest, the three students are executed by guillotine. A voice-over closes the film by informing the audience that a copy of the sixth pamphlet was smuggled out of Germany to England and was later dropped by the Allies over Germany as the 'Manifesto of the Munich Students' ('Manifest der Münchner Studenten'). The film concludes with images of the pamphlets falling from the skies over Munich.

When approaching any historical film — even films that open, as is the case of Rothemund's *Sophie Scholl*, with a statement announcing, 'This film is based on historical facts, as yet unpublished transcripts, and new interviews with witnesses'[5] — *what* is depicted should always be of secondary importance to *how* ideas are depicted and *why* that approach is important for understanding both the source material and the period in which the film was produced and released. Deviations from the historical record can be significant. Indeed, as we will see with the ending of *Sophie Scholl*, changes can serve to obfuscate rather than facilitate the audience's understanding

---

[5] 'Dieser Film beruht auf historischen Fakten, bisher unveröffentlichten Verhöhrprotokollen und neuen Interviews mit Zeitzeugen'.

of complex events. However, we should be careful not to hold historical films to an artificial standard of what constitutes an 'appropriate' treatment of the past. While it is true that films streamline and simplify events to make them 'feature-length', we should neither imply that written history offers an objective version of events, nor overlook what film as an audio-visual medium is uniquely placed to do, namely to 'add movement, colour, sound, and drama to the past'.[6] As Robert Rosenstone argues,

> the history film not only challenges traditional history, but helps return us to a kind of ground zero, a sense that we can never really know the past, but can only continually play with, reconfigure, and try to make meaning out of the traces it has left behind.[7]

Instead of simply highlighting historical 'errors', we should instead explore how the filmic medium is employed to engage audiences with the White Rose story and what the implications of these artistic interventions are for both our modern-day image of Sophie Scholl and for the film's theme of resistance more broadly.

Rothemund's film bears the hallmarks of a twenty-first-century re-examination of a figure who, just two years before the film's release, became only the second woman to be inducted into the Walhalla hall of fame, 'a place of remembrance for German-speaking men and women of outstanding merit as an inspiration and

---

[6] Robert A. Rosenstone, *History on Film/Film on History* (London: Routledge, 2006), p. 37.

[7] Idem., *History on Film/Film on History*, 2nd edn (Harlow, UK: Pearson, 2012), p. 186.

reference point for the nation'.[8] Two factors motivated Rothemund's decision to direct *Sophie Scholl*, his first historical film: the public interest in Scholl that surrounded the sixtieth anniversary of her execution in 2003, and the discovery of the original records from the Gestapo's interrogation of Scholl and of handwritten notes by Roland Freisler, in the former East German Ministry for State Security (Stasi) and SED party archives.[9] These documents only became available after German reunification and the incorporation of these materials sets Rothemund's film apart from the earlier depictions of Sophie Scholl.[10] At the same time, Rothemund was careful to point out that audiences 'should not feel that they are sitting in a history class' and he had no desire to 'make copies of historical scenes'.[11] Rather, he sought to bring the historical figure of Sophie Scholl closer to modern-day audiences by juxtaposing her experiences with current issues.[12] Here we find the emergence of

---

[8] Bayerische Verwaltung der staatlichen Schlösser, Gärten und Seen, 'Walhalla. Donaustauf Near Regensburg' <www.schloesser.bayern.de/englisch/palace/objects/walhalla.htm> [accessed 2 May 2019].

[9] The Sozialistische Einheitspartei Deutschlands (Socialist Unity Party of Germany) was the governing party of the German Democratic Republic between 1949 and 1990.

[10] According to Hans-Bernhard Moeller, Michael Verhoeven had seen the Gestapo records when developing his 1982 film, *Die Weiße Rose*. Verhoeven was friends with Anneliese Knoop-Graf, the sister of White Rose member Willi Graf. She had been granted access to the documents by Erich Honecker and later made these available to Verhoeven. See Hans-Bernard Moeller, 'Sophie Scholl and Post-WWII German Film: Resistance and the Third Wave', *Colloquia Germanica* 40 (2007), 19–35 (p. 31).

[11] Zeitgeist Film, '*Sophie Scholl — The Final Days*'. Press Notes, <https://zeitgeistfilms.com/media/films/136/sophiescholl.presskit.pdf> [accessed 1 May 2019].

[12] Ibid.

three key themes: the presentation of resistance, the implications of the decision to focus almost exclusively on the figure of Sophie Scholl, and — symptomatic of the sudden increase in films set in the Third Reich at the turn of the century — how Scholl is presented as a hero for the twenty-first century.

Extraordinarily Ordinary Resistance

The theme of resistance is introduced in the very opening moments of *Sophie Scholl*. The film begins with the sound of Billie Holiday's 'Sugar' playing on the radio. After a few seconds, the black screen fades in to reveal two young women in extreme close-up. We see both in turn before the camera selects the character who will become the focus for the film: Sophie. Suddenly, Sophie catches sight of her watch and states 'I have to go' ('Ich muss gehen'). This short and seemingly unremarkable opening subtly establishes the nature of the film's presentation of resistance. The image of two friends excitedly singing along to a song on the radio and trying to learn the lyrics is a scene with which many people can identify. Within the context of National Socialist Germany, however, these actions acquire a more profound significance. Sophie and Gisela are, in fact, singing along to a black 'degenerate' jazz song banned under National Socialism.[13] When Sophie realises she must leave, she stands up to turn off the radio. Her body partially obscures her actions, but we can hear her not only turn off the radio, but also carefully change the station. They have been listening to a *Feindsender* ('enemy radio station'), the

---

[13] 'Degenerate' ('entartet') was a term applied to different forms of art that were labelled 'un-German' and corrupting through the social, cultural, 'racial', or political identities of their creators.

BBC, and Sophie conceals this by changing the station back to a licit one.

Sophie Scholl is a film about resistance. However, whereas resistance films in the Federal Republic overwhelmingly focused on the actions of military elites (in particular Claus von Stauffenberg and Wilhelm Canaris), and East German films frequently celebrated the role of the antifascist resistance, *Sophie Scholl* places the spotlight on the small-scale actions of students. In this regard, the poster for the English-language release of the film introduces a tantalising, and yet also somewhat misleading, scenario: 'The true story of a strong woman who did what few in Nazi Germany dared even think'. The resistance acts undertaken by Sophie and the White Rose are remarkable precisely because of how everyday they seem: from listening to banned music on an illegal radio station to writing and distributing pamphlets. In this way, Sophie's question to Hans as they prepare to go to the university to distribute the pamphlets — 'inconspicuous enough?' ('unauffällig genug?') — characterises the type of resistance undertaken by the group as a whole.

The desire to foreground both the low-level resistance offered by the group and the decision to focus on the only woman among the six core members of the White Rose is integral to the film's repositioning of what it means to resist. When Mohr accuses Sophie of making derogatory statements about the state's abuse of power, she replies angrily, 'Derogatory is calling my brother and me criminals because of some pamphlets! We've only tried to convince people with words.'[14] Mohr and Freisler have responses to the political indictments contained in the White Rose's pamplets, but they have no response to the moral accusations levelled against them by Sophie. The moral divide separating Sophie from the representatives of the National Socialist state is exemplified in a scene during the trial that was widely used in the film's promotional materials. The camera is positioned over the shoulder of Freisler and we see the courtroom from his perspective. Sophie is facing the camera. Every seat in the courtroom is occupied by members of the SS and state ministers. The scene composition brings into focus the remarkable reversal of societal, legal, and moral norms under National Socialism: a twenty-one-year-old student responsible for circulating anti-war pamphlets stands accused of treason by a state responsible for the active perpetration of war crimes.

The scene also foregrounds the film's targeted use of desaturated colour grading. Against a dominant background of greys and browns, the colour red is strategically used throughout the film to contrast key figures and ideas. Red is first used to single out Sophie, through her red cardigan. Her increasing vulnerability over the course of the film is signalled through the introduction of red items associated with the power of the state: the red cover of the German Penal Code (*Strafgesetzbuch*) on Mohr's desk, the red of the Gestapo officer's bowtie, and the red of the National Socialist banners in the Gestapo headquarters and in the courtroom. As Sophie stands in the court before Freisler, the red of her cardigan is framed by the red of

---

[14] '*Sie* reden abfällig, wenn Sie meinen Bruder und mich wegen ein paar Flugblätter Verbrecher nennen, obwohl wir nichts anderes machen, als mit Worten zu überzeugen versuchen.'

Freisler's robes in front of her and the red of the National Socialist banner behind her. Yet despite the vulnerability of the young woman at the hands of the state, she returns Freisler's gaze resolutely: it is the red associated with Sophie that commands our attention, not the red of the National Socialist state.

The courtroom scene also highlights a second, more problematic, point. The red of the National Socialist banner also draws attention to the otherwise conspicuous absence of National Socialist insignia. Other than in the courtroom, there are very few examples of swastikas or National Socialist uniforms, or instances of characters offering the Nazi salute (*Hitlergruß*). This was a deliberate strategy by the director, who chose to avoid overt visual signifiers of the period in order to 'cut down the distance' between the modern-day spectator and the past so that audiences could 'slip right into the action'.[15] While the desire to convey the moral need to act to a contemporary audience is an undoubted strength of *Sophie Scholl*, the film nonetheless takes a highly politicised and complex period of history and largely strips it of its specificity. Not only does this result in a clear tension between the opening assertion of the film's historical credentials and its oddly ahistorical engagement with the past, it also denies the audience a wider context in which to understand the group's actions.

Here we encounter a perennial problem faced when analysing the historical film: to what extent is it the duty of a filmmaker to inform and even instruct an audience about a historical period? Is a filmmaker's primary duty to fulfil the narrative and visual requirements of the filmic medium, or does a filmmaker have a duty

---

[15] Zeitgeist Film, '*Sophie Scholl — The Final Days*'.

to the historical source material as well? And to what extent are these questions further complicated by the opening text that invites the audience to understand the action as historically accurate? There are no straightforward answers to these questions. At no point has Rothemund claimed to have made the definitive story of Scholl or her final days. Nonetheless, within the context of a film that thematises the actions of students who circulated anti-war pamphlets under National Socialism in Germany in the early 1940s, it is important to ask what we actually learn about the content of the pamphlets, the context of the group's decision to act, or their individual motivations for resisting.

'She was not born a Hero'

Interviews with Rothemund reveal that the decision to focus on Sophie Scholl in particular was driven by the image of resistance she offered. Sophie was not the most important member of the group, nor was she the most politically engaged. Whereas Hans was 'the political head from the very start, an intellectual, a fighter' (' der politische Kopf von Anfang an, ein Intellektueller, ein Kämpfer'), Sophie offered a far more everyday image of a resister.[16] Moreover, the director was keen to stress that Sophie 'was not born a hero' ('Sie ist nicht als Heldin geboren'), but rather was an 'engaged, young woman' as well as a 'completely normal student' ('nicht nur die engagierte junge Frau, sondern auch die ganz normale Studentin.').[17]

---

[16] Margret Köhler, 'Warum erneut ein Film über Sophie Scholl? Gespräch mit dem Regisseur Marc Rothemund', Bundeszentrale für politische Bildung, 20 April 2005 <http://www.bpb.de/geschichte/nationalsozialismus/weisse-rose/61078/interview-mit-regisseur-marc-rothemund> [accessed 1 May 2019].
[17] Ibid.

The episodes in-between the interrogations with Mohr during which Sophie talks to her cellmate, Else Gebel, play a crucial role in conveying the 'more human and fragile side' to Sophie.[18] In these exchanges, Sophie appears far less self-assured. It is here we see her cry, express considerable concern about her mother and fiancé, worry about the future, and, at one point, howl with despair. The audience is further encouraged to see the 'human side' of the long-celebrated resistance hero through the use of medium and close-up shots coupled with occasional point-of view shots.

While these moments undoubtedly contribute to a 'stronger [...] identification with her fate, her attitude, her arguments, and emotions', visually the film repeatedly employs tropes that risk undercutting the depiction of Sophie as an everyday figure who is relatable to audiences today.[19] The depiction of Sophie has been one of the more criticised aspects of the film. Contrary to the director's aim of presenting Sophie as a readily identifiable figure, a number of critics have pointed to the film's tendency to render her a 'quasi-religious hero'.[20] Here again we return to the need to differentiate

---

[18] Owen Evans, '"Wonderfully Courageous"?: The Human Face of a Legend in *Sophie Scholl: Die letzten Tage/Sophie Scholl: The Final Days* (2005)', in *New Directions in German Cinema*, ed. by Paul Cooke and Chris Homewood (London: I.B. Tauris, 2011), pp. 57–76 (p. 67).

[19] 'Damit verbinden wir den Zuschauer so eng es geht mit unserer Hauptfigur. Je enger die Bindung, umso höher die Identifikation mit ihrem Schicksal, ihrer Haltung, ihren Argumenten und Emotionen.' Fred Breinersdorfer, *Sophie Scholl — Die letzten Tage* (Frankfurt a.M.: Fischer Taschenbuch Verlag, 2006), p. 317 (my translation).

[20] Hartwig Tegeler, 'Mythenbildung auf der Leinwand', *Deutschlandfunk Kultur*, 19 July 2014 <https://www.deutschlandfunkkultur.de/geschichte-mythenbildung-auf-der-leinwand.1270.de.html?dram:article_id=292174> [accessed 1 May 2019] (my translation).

between *what* is depicted and *how* it is depicted. The repeated motif of Sophie looking out of windows with her eyes directed to the sky points to an inner experience and religious conviction that the film never fully vocalises. Furthermore, the tendency to bathe Sophie in light which, when coupled with the use of greys and browns in the film, accentuates her status as a remarkable figure and symbolises her exceptionalism. The tension between the narrative and visual presentation of Sophie is also exemplified by how she speaks. Sophie spoke with a Swabian accent, but according to Julia Jentsch (who plays Sophie in the film), the decision was taken to present her without the regional accent as that 'would have created a distance and caused a certain perplexity that we wanted to avoid at all costs.'[21] Collectively, the decisions to remove Sophie's regional accent and to employ a symbolism that evokes religious martyrdom conversely risk distancing the audience from the image of an everyday woman that the film seeks to promote.

A Twenty-First-Century Hero

The desire to present Sophie as a figure with whom modern-day audiences could readily identify was part of a wider strategy designed to broaden the appeal and demonstrate the ongoing significance of Sophie's actions beyond the context of the Third Reich. According to the film's screenwriter Fred Breinersdorfer:

> We are living in a time in which fascist parties in Europe are on the march again and in Germany far-right parties are being elected to parliaments — predominantly by young voters. Everywhere people are complaining that young people do not have any role models. But at the

---

[21] Zeitgeist Film, '*Sophie Scholl — The Final Days*'.

same time, pupils are staying away from classes in order to protest about the Iraq War and colourful flags bearing the word 'peace' are fluttering in windows and on balconies. A film about Sophie Scholl, about the final moments of a young woman full of life, about her growth under increasing pressure, about the ramifications of her stance, is necessary in times like these.[22]

The focus on individuals who 'fought Hitler with words and not with violence' ('Hitler nur mit Worten und nicht mit Gewalt bekämpfte') as well as on individuals, especially women, who have traditionally been marginalised figures within resistance narratives, is indicative of the filmmakers' discussion of what is meant by resistance. Through the figure of Sophie Scholl, they are able to demonstrate both the heroic actions of the White Rose and the extent to which moral activism orientated towards non-violent resistance has a rightful place in the public view, on screen, and in historical books.[23]

Breinersdorfer's screenplay selects material from the protocols of Sophie's interrogation and presents them as a thirty-three-minute dialogue which, crucially, is supplemented by

---

[22] 'Wir leben in einer Zeit, in der faschistische Parteien in Europa wieder trommeln und in Deutschland rechtsradikale Parteien in die Parlamente gewählt werden — überwiegend von jungen Wählern. Überall wird beklagt, die Jugend habe keine Vorbilder. Doch gleichzeitig bleiben Schüler dem Unterricht fern, um gegen den Krieg im Irak zu demonstrieren, und bunte Fahnen mit der Aufschrift „Peace" flattern an Fenstern und Balkonen. Ein Film über Sophie Scholl, über den letzten Weg einer lebensfrohen jungen Frau, über ihr Wachsen unter zunehmendem Druck, über die Konsequenz ihrer Haltung, ist notwendig in einer solchen Zeit.' Breinersdorfer, *Sophie Scholl*, p. 317 (my translation).

[23] Ibid., p. 316.

additional dialogue taken from interviews, witness statements, Sophie's own writings, and the group's pamphlets. While the use of multiple sources undeniably offers audiences a more comprehensive image of Sophie, it also risks overstating Sophie's *individual* impact in the past and present. At one point in her final interrogation, Sophie points to the role of young people (the film's target audience) in ensuring a new Germany and Europe: 'The German name will be forever defamed if young Germans do not finally arise [...] and raise up a new intellectual Europe' ('Der deutsche Name bleibt für immer geschändet, wenn nicht die deutsche Jugend endlich aufsteht [...] und ein neues geistiges Europa aufrichtet.'). The line is taken directly from the White Rose's sixth pamphlet and was not written by Sophie, but by a key figure who is conspicuously absent from the film: Professor Kurt Huber. [24] Although Breinersdorfer has openly discussed the multiple uses of sources in interviews, it is not clear when and where in the film alternative voices are attributed to Sophie. The inclusion of such statements is indicative of the desire to position Sophie as a figure of identification for a young, postwar generation. In doing so, however, the film arguably overstates the extent of Sophie's individual contribution to the group's aims.

The desire to draw clear links between Sophie's actions during the Third Reich and the future of post-war Germany can also be seen in the film's closing scenes. After Sophie, Hans, and Christoph are sentenced to death, they are taken to the execution chamber. Sophie is carried to the guillotine. As she is positioned face

---

[24] Huber's name is listed at the end of the film as one of the group members who was also executed for his activities with the White Rose, although no further detail is given regarding what these actions were.

down, her face fills the frame in an extreme close-up shot and her eyes stare resolutely into the camera. The camera cuts to the falling guillotine blade and the screen fades to black. The diegetic sound continues, and we hear Hans and Christoph being brought into the chamber and executed. The screen remains black for seventy-five seconds before the names of the White Rose members who were executed and imprisoned are listed on screen. The silence is broken by a voice-over, which reveals that Helmuth von Moltke smuggled the sixth pamphlet to England and that millions of copies were dropped by the Allies over Germany.[25] The final image of the film is of pieces of white paper falling from the skies around Munich. The scene immediately evokes two earlier episodes: as the camera tilts upward to the piercing sunlight, we are reminded of Sophie's frequent gazing up at the sky, and the falling pamphlets recall when Sophie pushed the pamphlets off the balcony. The film places the airdrop in 'mid-1943'. Although Allied bombing raids would not target Munich until spring 1944, the cityscape nonetheless bears no markers of the war. Instead, the film presents a somewhat timeless picture of Munich, and crucially, one that is readily identifiable to modern-day audiences.[26]

---

[25] The decision to name von Moltke explicitly is somewhat odd given the film never establishes who he was. He was a member of the *Kreisauer Kreis* (Kreisau Circle), a group of Germans opposed to the National Socialist regime. While the group never engaged in resistance activities, their actions were considered treasonous by the state. Von Moltke was executed in January 1945.

[26] Originally, the film ended with quotations attributed to Thomas Mann and Winston Churchill. These were removed in the final edit, thereby restoring the focus on Sophie's words and actions.

Conclusion

Sophie Scholl — Die letzten Tage is an important landmark in the representation of the White Rose on film. Rothemund goes further than Verhoeven and Adlon in embedding the historical record of the Gestapo interrogations within the filmic narrative, and in bringing the audience so close to the individual figure of Sophie, not just as a resister, but also as a young woman. In this way, the film seeks to cast light on resistance acts in the Third Reich and, in the process, makes an appeal for moral engagement and activism in the present. This approach is not without its problems. The focus on Sophie's moral over political convictions risks decontextualizing her actions in the past and over-emphasising the direct impact of the group's (and specifically Sophie's) legacy after 1945. These points aside, however, the film shows the bravery of individuals who were motivated by their moral beliefs and the disproportionate brutality of the state's reponse. As a film released at a turning point in post-war memory, when direct access to those who knew Sophie Scholl and the White Rose members, and indeed those who experienced the period first-hand, began to contract, *Sophie Scholl* demonstrates to a new generation of audiences the importance of the moral agency of an individual and the need to speak out against injustice.

Elizabeth Ward is a Lecturer in German in the School of Histories, Languages and Cultures at the University of Hull. Her research interests include the Holocaust on film, East German cinema, and Cold War German cinema. Elizabeth has published on East German Holocaust film and the historical film in twenty-first-century German cinema. Her current research project examines the relationship between film festivals and cultural diplomacy in Cold War Germany.

THE WHITE ROSE PAMPHLETS

TRANSLATORS' INTRODUCTION

Zoë Aebischer, Sophie Bailey, Ilona Clayton, Ro Crawford,
Pauline Gümpel, Eve Mason, Adam Mazarelo, Louise Mayer-
Jacquelin, Timothy Powell, Finn Provan, Poppy Robertson,
Emily Rowland, Harry Smith, Amy Wilkinson,
Madeleine Williamson-Sarll.

Over the course of eight months, from October to May 2019, we worked together to produce a new translation of the White Rose resistance pamphlets. We approached this project from a number of different backgrounds and perspectives. Some of us had studied the White Rose at school, through Marc Rothemund's film *Sophie Scholl — Die letzten Tage* (*Sophie Scholl — The Final Days*, 2005), while for others it was a name and a story that had been encountered only vaguely. Few of us had read the pamphlets, and this project offered the opportunity to approach the White Rose from a linguistic, as well as an historical, perspective. Here, we outline our response to the texts and the approaches we took as translators.

Our translation was a collaborative project. This proved to be a fruitful and exciting way to work. 'As well as mirroring the way the leaflets were originally written', Amy Wilkinson writes, 'translating in a team meant that there were always several solutions we could pick from, resulting in the best translation possible'. The result was that frequently, the process of exchange and peer review made us think about the texts in new ways. As Pauline Gümpel comments: 'Especially when bearing in mind that the White Rose itself was a group of students, working together on these texts, I feel very grateful for this opportunity to discuss possible phrasings for our translation with my peers and hear their thoughts.' Our experience translating this material necessitated reflection on the kind of texts the pamphlets are, and how we as students approach them in a unique way. For example, Ro Crawford emphasises the affinity between student activism in the past and the present: 'A lot has changed in the seventy-five years since the White Rose group was active, but the social and political activism concentrated at universities is still a big part of the student experience for many of us.' Unlike the White Rose members, however, as Madeleine Williamson-Sarll points out, 'we could work on the leaflets without the fear of discovery and return to our studies knowing that we were in no danger'.

Translating as a group meant we had to come to decisions collectively, which included agreeing on standard terms for words that recur throughout the six pamphlets. This sometimes proved difficult. Ilona Clayton writes: 'I loved going over the pamphlets with everyone, but sometimes it felt like we were going in circles because everyone preferred different things.' Even the word 'Flugblatt' was disputed, as Emily Rowland explains: 'The publishing of "Flugblätter" is an established tradition in the German-speaking world, but the word does not have a direct English-language equivalent.' Although 'leaflet' is often used to refer to the White Rose's 'Flugblätter', we finally decided to use the word 'pamphlet' because of its political connotations.

We were also aware of the very particular context in which the pamphlets were written and disseminated. This was not like doing a translation in a tutorial, where we usually work on an extract from a text, complete a version individually, and receive feedback (principally) from a tutor. Gümpel writes that she felt 'a particular kind of responsibility to try and convey the historical reality as accurately as possible, which was different from all the translations I had done before.' Similarly, for Crawford,

> one of the most striking aspects of the language of the originals is how jarring it is; it's easy to dismiss the drama of their work as proof of the White Rose members' youth, passion and idealism — and they certainly represent all of those things — but there's also the crushing reminder that for these young people, their activism really was a matter of life and death.

Sophie Bailey adds: 'When translating the White Rose, I felt very strongly the weight attached to their words and the importance of translating them as accurately as possible, whilst still preserving their original beauty and power.'

The language of the pamphlets threw up several challenges. The style changes, as Williamson-Sarll notes, 'partly due to who wrote them, but also due to the increasing sense of urgency'. We can also discern the influence of other individuals in the wider circle of the White Rose.[1] Williamson-Sarll adds that we were faced with a 'text-book' translation problem:

> if we wanted to stay completely true to the originals, our versions might also sound bizarre and jarring, and might look like a 'bad' translation. But if we succumbed to the

---

[1] One example is the writer and translator Theodor Haecker (1879-1945), whose influence is traceable in the fourth pamphlet. It draws on theology and metaphysics, presenting Hitler as the Antichrist.

temptation of over-correction, we would be producing something different, which was not our intention.

We aimed to produce an equivalent effect in our English translation as was created by the German. This applied to individual words and phrases, and to the overall style of the texts. Zoë Aebischer explains:

> Sometimes we translated a sentence, but when spoken out loud it didn't carry the same ring as the German, or ended weakly, or lost some of its emphatic nature, which then required less literal translation solutions.

We also had to agree on the kind of style and register we wanted for our English versions. Crawford explains that we had to decide whether 'to put the English versions into today's vernacular or attempt to make the language authentic to the time of writing.' We had a choice: to aim our translations at twenty-first-century readers, or for the audience for which the group was writing in the early 1940s. We prioritised what Finn Provan summarises as 'voice, nuance, and raw intention' and tried to ignore 'our privileged position of hindsight'. We had to bear in mind too that as Timothy Powell notes, 'The elevated language the group used conveys their idealistic view of humankind's capacity for good as well as for evil.' We did not want to lose this aspect of the texts. Eve Mason writes: 'it was important to us as a group to convey the vigour, the emotion behind the words of the pamphlets. These were students who wanted more than anything to provoke action, to inspire resistance, and this meant we prioritised tone and emotion over pedantic linguistic accuracy.'

Another challenge was dealing with the intertextuality embedded in the original pamphlets, especially biblical references.

Crawford explains that such references 'often required research to find both the sources and the wording of these other texts where they appeared in existing translations that would be familiar to an English-speaking audience'. The pamphlets also quote from a range of writers and philosophers. Gümpel writes of the second pamphlet,

> the translation of a passage by Laozi sounded very awkward and old-fashioned in German and it was therefore difficult to make a decision about the extent to which this should be 'improved' in English.

Indeed, the quotations made us more aware of the 'group's desire to draw on authors and philosophers who had influenced them, but this often came across as out-of-place, as if they were desperate to make use of anything and everything they had read and studied' (Williamson-Sarll).

One of the most significant challenges was to translate especially 'German' terms which do not have straightforward English-language equivalents. The word 'Geist', for example was problematic. Powell explains that it is 'a highly complex philosophical and religious concept deeply rooted in German philosophy, particularly Enlightenment discourse' and that 'it was difficult to find an equivalent in English philosophy (intellect would probably be the best word we have but it's not perfect for a number of reasons)'. Zoë Aebischer adds that even a word like 'Staat', used particularly in the third pamphlet, was tricky, because 'in English "state" can have a different meaning; sometimes we used "government" to make it clearer.' On the difficulty of translating 'Staat', Williamson-Sarll adds

In some places, the translation as 'state' was unproblematic and made sense, but in other paragraphs the implication seemed to be 'government' rather than 'state'. This led to a discussion of the difference between the two, and we had to consider whether leaving it in the German would in fact be less misleading. 'Unstaat' was of course even more problematic, given that there is no obvious English equivalent.

Another challenge was posed by words which had been part of Nazi propaganda. The word 'Volk', as Powell explains, 'has been rooted in German philosophical/political/religious discourse since the late Middle Ages'. Gümpel adds

> It is hard to express the role it took on in the context of Nazi society, and also, how it has changed throughout history, for example by being included in the 1989 reunification slogan 'Wir sind das Volk!'.

The authors' use of such terms also reflects their understanding of the regime, as Powell points out: 'they demonstrated a high level of awareness and understanding of the failings of National Socialist ideology by using the regime's own ideological language against it.' This is particularly clear in the second pamphlet, when the Nazis are referred to with the word 'Untermenschentum' ('sub-humanity'), a term they themselves were using to refer to those they considered racially inferior.

We encountered some instances where we had to resign ourselves to 'loss' in translating the texts from German to English. Crawford notes that the word 'Verführer', which appears in the fifth pamphlet, 'seems much more powerful than the English "corruptor", and echoes the Nazi term "Führer" used for Hitler; there was no way for us to preserve the relationship between the words that the German manages so neatly.' Zoë Aebischer writes:

> we had to decide where it would be more appropriate to use a more literal translation or to use a more interpretative translation to make our version more accessible. One example in the third pamphlet is the simile of guilt rising 'gleich einer parabolischen Kurve' (literally: 'like a parabolic curve') — it is as if they had been studying parabolic curves in class. I'm proud of our solution of 'guilt growing exponentially', as it is still linked with maths, but conveys the meaning in a clearer way.

We also wanted to address the fact that existing translations did not seem to go far enough in conveying the gender inclusivity of the texts which, as Mason points out, is not insignificant. For example, the sixth pamphlet addresses student readers with the words 'Kommilitoninnen! Kommilitonen!' (literally: 'fellow female and male students!'). Mason adds that the White Rose group was 'genuinely calling out to "alle Deutsche" ("all Germans")' and adds that 'where German can employ the gender neutral "man" ("one") or "Mensch" ("human"/"person"), we have tried to translate this wherever possible using "they" rather than "he".'[2] This also struck us as a way of emphasising the importance of women's role within the resistance, including Sophie Scholl's contribution. Mason argues:

---

[2] There was one instance where this didn't work, in the sixth pamphlet: 'Even the most dull-witted German has had his eyes opened by the terrible bloodbath, which, in the name of the freedom and honour of the German nation, they have unleashed upon Europe, and unleash anew each day.'

Within a university context where female students were being attacked by Nazi leaders as 'well-bred daughters' who were shirking their war duties by studying at university, and being told that 'the natural place for a woman is not at the university, but with her family, at the side of her husband',[3] Sophie Scholl's bravery not only to further her education, but to resist the tyranny of the Third Reich, must be celebrated. Neither should the work of many women within the periphery of the White Rose group, who supported the six core members, be overlooked.

We decided to include a brief glossary of terms with recur throughout the pamphlets, and endnotes so that readers could access further information but could also read the pamphlets as stand-alone texts without further commentary if they wished. We hope that readers who do not speak German may find a way into the language through out translations, using the parallel text and the supporting materials as a guide.

We hope our translation will reach a wide audience, including new readers who have perhaps never heard of the White Rose, or only have vague ideas about what it was and did. Bailey writes: 'Now, more than ever, the words of the White Rose are relevant and necessary, and I hope that our translation can give them a new lease of life.' Rowland adds that 'In times of growing uncertainty and tension, it is important that these texts are not forgotten, and that they continue to generate meaningful

---

[3] Paul Giesler, 13 January 1943, University of Munich, cited in Russell Freedman, *We Will Not Be Silent: The White Rose Student Resistance Movement That Defied Adolf Hitler* (New York: Clarion Books, 2016), p. 65.

discussions.' For some of us, reading the pamphlets so closely over a considerable period of time, gave us a new perspective on this period of history. Gümpel writes of the emotional connection she developed with the material:

> I am deeply moved by the thought that Sophie Scholl was the same age as I am now when she made the decision to become part of the resistance against the Nazis — a decision that she paid for with her life. I hope that especially students will read these translations and that these translated texts will have a similar effect of bringing this part of German history emotionally closer to them, just as it brought the texts closer to me.

The translation project also led to some fascinating insights into writing and resistance more broadly, as Adam Mazarelo explains:

> During the Arab Spring, disabled mobile and internet networks meant activists turned to leaflets as a means of highlighting and railing against the current and historical abuses of dictatorial regimes. In the Egyptian case, many of these leaflets were scanned and made available as part of a collection called the Taḥrīr Documents. Reading these leaflets now, eight years later and with the White Rose in mind, it's impossible not to hear the echoes across time. Drawing, as the White Rose did, on cultural and religious heritage they saw themselves as defending against perversion and erasure, the printed ephemera of the revolutions of 2011 are just as rich in satire, irony and anger. In both cases, moreover, the words ring just as true for the leaflets' contemporary readers as they do today.

Finally, the process of translating this material has led to important reflections on the power of the written word and the potential young people especially have to stand up against injustice. As Mason concludes,

> In an age in which young people are constantly being accused of apolitical cynicism, I hope our translation of these pamphlets can provide an example to the youth of today of the political action our generation can achieve and of the true potential we have to make a change in the world.

Glossary

We have included a brief explanation of some key terms which recur thoughout the pamphlets.

Freiheit. The German word for freedom, which features especially heavily in the sixth leaflet, in the phrase 'Freiheit und Ehre' ('freedom and honour'). The repetition makes this something of a rallying call, as the White Rose call for the freedom of the individual. They imply that the love of freedom is intrinsically German, evoking a German literary and philosophical tradition which includes Goethe and Kant. Goethe's famous knight-hero in his play *Götz von Berlichingen* (1773) embodies these values, refusing to bow to an unjust authority and fighting to protect German independence. Götz dies in prison with the last word 'Freiheit'. Hans Scholl's last words were 'Es lebe die Freiheit!' ('Long live freedom!').

Mitläufer. A 'fellow-traveller', one who follows a group without particularly supporting or even liking it, instead becoming a hanger-on through opportunism or lack of courage. The term was widely used in the Nuremberg Trials and throughout the post-war period to denote 'followers': those who were considered lesser offenders in the Nazi hierarchy, but were still not wholly exonerated. Hannah Arendt provides a good summary of the sense of being a 'Mitläufer' in *Eichmann in Jerusalem* (1963), where she describes how the Nazi regime made it easier to do wrong than right: 'Evil in the Third Reich had lost the quality by which most people recognize it — the quality of temptation. Many Germans and many Nazis, probably an overwhelming majority of them, must have been tempted not to murder, not to rob, not to let their neighbours go off to their doom [...], and not to become accomplices in all these crimes by benefiting from them. But, God knows, they had learned to resist temptation.'[4]

Mitschuld. The term 'Mitschuld' is a compound of the words 'Schuld', meaning 'guilt' or 'fault', and the prefix 'Mit-' ('with'). Thus, it expresses an individual's share in someone else's guilt. The notion of 'Mitschuld' had great importance in the post-war discussion of Germans' responsibility, as it is used to express the idea that the individuals within a society, which allows deeds like the Nazi atrocities to happen, share the blame for these actions. In the second pamphlet, the White Rose claim that all Germans who do not protest against the Nazi regime must feel this kind of collective guilt.

---

[4] Hannah Arendt, *Eichmann in Jerusalem: A Report on the Banality of Evil*, ed. by Amos Elon (London: Penguin, 2005), p. 150.

Staat. Broadly corresponds to the English 'state' with more emphasis on the mechanism of government (as in the adjectival sense of 'state' in 'state pension', for example). It can also refer to the nation as a whole. Here it has frequently been translated as 'state' or 'government', in the latter case often for clarity, and to avoid the ambiguity of the English, where state can also mean 'condition'. Two 'untranslatable' cases in the pamphlets are 'Unstaat' in the third pamphlet and 'Terrorstaat' in the fourth, which have been rendered as 'false state' and 'terror state' respectively. 'Unstaat' is somewhat stronger than 'false state', as the German prefix Un- can also be applied to nouns to denote an antithesis: the noun 'Unheil', for example, meaning evil, calamity or affliction, comprises the prefix and the noun 'Heil', meaning spiritual or physical wellbeing. As such, 'Unstaat' indicates that the Nazi regime is not only 'false', but also antithetical to what it should mean to be a state.

Volk. A term meaning 'nation' or 'people' originally used by the nationalist *völkisch* movement, which had its roots in the late nineteenth century and resurfaced after the First World War in opposition to liberal democracy under the Weimar Republic. The movement's racist and anti-semitic attitudes and its ideal of the creation of a nation state based on a supposed common German ethnicity strongly influenced National Socialist racial ideology. The National Socialists used 'Das deutsche Volk' as an umbrella term for everybody whom they considered to be 'ethnically German', including those who lived outside of Germany.

Figure 4. Poster designed and printed by student translators at the Bodleian's Bibliographical Press.

THE FIRST PAMPHLET

Summer 1942

Flugblätter der Weissen Rose.

I

Nichts ist eines Kulturvolkes unwürdiger, als sich ohne Widerstand von einer verantwortungslosen und dunklen Trieben ergebenen Herrscherclique "regieren" zu lassen. Ist es nicht so, dass sich jeder ehrliche Deutsche heute seiner Regierung schämt, und wer von uns ahnt das Ausmass der Schmach, die über uns und unsere Kinder kommen wird, wenn einst der Schleier von unseren Augen gefallen ist und die grauenvollsten und jegliches Mass unendlich überschreitenden Verbrechen ans Tageslicht treten? Wenn das deutsche Volk schon so in seinem tiefsten Wesen korrumpiert und zerfallen ist, dass es ohne eine Hand zu regen, im leichtsinnigen Vertrauen auf eine fragwürdige Gesetzmässigkeit der Geschichte, das Höchste, das ein Mensch besitzt, und das ihn über jede andere Kreatur erhöht, nämlich den freien Willen, preisgibt, die Freiheit des Menschen preisgibt, selbst mit einzugreifen in das Rad der Geschichte und es seiner vernünftigen Entscheidung unterzuordnen, wenn die Deutschen so jeder Individualität bar, schon so sehr zur geistlosen und feigen Masse geworden sind, dann, ja dann verdienen sie den Untergang.

Goethe spricht von den Deutschen als einem tragischen Volke, gleich dem der Juden und Griechen, aber heute hat es eher den Anschein, als sei es eine seichte, willenlose Herde von Mitläufern, denen das Mark aus dem Innersten gesogen und nun ihres Kernes beraubt, bereit sind sich in den Untergang hetzen zu lassen. Es scheint so - aber es ist nicht so; vielmehr hat man in langsamer, trügerischer, systematischer Vergewaltigung jeden einzelnen in ein geistiges Gefängnis gesteckt, und erst, als er darin gefesselt lag, wurde er sich des Verhängnisses bewusst. Wenige nur erkannten das drohende Verderben, und der Lohn für ihr heroisches Mahnen war der Tod. Ueber das Schicksal dieser Menschen wird noch zu reden sein.

Wenn jeder wartet, bis der Andere anfängt, werden die Boten der rächenden Nemesis unaufhaltsam näher und näher rücken, dann wird auch das letzte Opfer sinnlos in den Rachen des unersättlichen Dämons geworfen sein. Daher muss jeder Einzelne seiner Verantwortung als Mitglied der christlichen und abendländischen Kultur bewusst in dieser letzten Stunde sich wehren so viel er kann, arbeiten wider die Geissel der Menschheit, wider den Faschismus und jedes ihm ähnliche System des absoluten Staates. Leistet passiven Widerstand - W i d e r s t a n d - wo immer Ihr auch seid, verhindert das Weiterlaufen dieser atheistischen Kriegsmaschine, ehe es zu spät ist, ehe die letzten Städte ein Trümmerhaufen sind, gleich Köln, und ehe die letzte Jugend des Volkes irgendwo für die Hybris eines Untermenschen verblutet ist. Vergesst nicht, dass ein jedes Volk diejenige Regierung verdient, die es erträgt!

Aus Friedrich Schiller, "Die Gesetzgebung des Lykurgus und Solon".

"....Gegen seinen eigenen Zweck gehalten, ist die Gesetzgebung des Lykurgus ein Meisterstück der Staats- und Menschenkunde. Er wollte einen mächtigen, in sich selbst gegründeten, unzerstörbaren Staat; politische Stärke und Dauerhaftigkeit waren das Ziel, wonach er strebte, und dieses Ziel hat er so weit erreicht, als unter seinen Umständen möglich war. Aber hält man den Zweck, welchen Lykurgus sich vorsetzte, gegen den Zweck der Menschheit, so muss eine tiefe Missbilligung an die Stelle der Bewunderung treten, die uns der erste, flüchtige Blick abgewonnen hat. Alles darf dem Besten des Staates zum Opfer gebracht werden, nur dasjenige nicht, dem der Staat selbst nur als ein Mittel dient. Der Staat selbst ist niemals Zweck, er ist nur wichtig als eine Bedingung, unter welcher der Zweck der Menschheit erfüllt werden kann, und dieser Zweck der Menschheit ist kein anderer, als Ausbildung aller Kräfte des Menschen, Fortschreitung. Hindert eine Staatsverfassung,dass alle Kräfte, die im Menschen liegen, sich entwickeln; hindert sie die Fortschreitung des Geistes, so ist sie verwerflich und schädlich, sie mag übrigens noch so durchdacht und in ihrer Art noch so vollkommen sein. Ihre Dauerhaftigkeit selbst gereicht ihr alsdann vielmehr zum Vorwurf, als zum Ruhme - sie ist dann nur ein verlängertes Uebel; je länger sie Bestand hat, umso schädlicher ist sie.

.....Auf Unkosten aller sittlichen Gefühle wurde das politische Verdienst errungen und die Fähigkeit dazu ausgebildet. In Sparta gab es keine eheliche Liebe, keine Mutterliebe, keine kindliche Liebe, keine Freundschaft - es gab nichts als Bürger, nichts als bürgerliche Tugend.

.....Ein Staatsgesetz machte den Spartanern die Unmenschlichkeit gegen ihre Sklaven zur Pflicht; in diesen unglücklichen Schlachtopfern wurde die Menschheit beschimpft und misshandelt. In dem spartanischen Gesetzbuche selbst wurde der gefährliche Grundsatz gepredigt, Menschen als Mittel und nicht als Zwecke zu betrachten - dadurch wurden die Grundfesten des Naturrechts und der Sittlichkeit gesetzmässig eingerissen.

.....Welch schöneres Schauspiel gibt der rauhe Krieger Cajus Marcius in seinem Lager vor Rom, der Rache und Sieg aufopfert, weil er die Tränen der Mutter nicht fliessen sehen kann!"

"...Der Staat (des Lykurgus) konnte nur unter der einzigen Bedingung fortdauern, wenn der Geist des Volks stillstünde; er konnte sich also nur dadurch erhalten, dass er den höchsten und einzigen Zweck eines Staates verfehlte."

Aus Goethe "Des Epimenides Erwachen", zweiter Aufzug, vierter Auftritt:

                     Genien

                      .....
          Doch was dem Abgrund kühn entstiegen,
          Kann durch ein ehernes Geschick
          Den halben Weltkreis übersiegen,
          Zum Abgrund muss es doch zurück.
          Schon droht ein ungeheures Bangen,
          Vergebens wird er widerstehn!
          Und alle, die noch an ihn hangen,
          Sie müssen mit zu Grunde gehn

                     Hoffnung

          Nun begegn' ich meinen Braven,
          Die sich in der Nacht versammelt
          Um zu schweigen, nicht zu schlafen,
          Und das schöne Wort der Freiheit
          Wird gelispelt und gestammelt,
          Bis in ungewohnter Neuheit
          Wir an unsrer Tempel Stufen
          Wieder neu entzückt es rufen:
                  (Mit Ueberzeugung laut.)
          Freiheit!
                      (gemässigter)
                      Freiheit!
                  (von allen Seiten und Enden Echo)
                      Freiheit!

          ──────────────────

Wir bitten Sie, dieses Blatt mit möglichst vielen Durchschlägen abzuschreiben und weiter zu verteilen!

Flugblätter der Weißen Rose I

Nichts ist eines Kulturvolkes unwürdiger, als sich ohne Widerstand von einer verantwortungslosen und dunklen Trieben ergebenen Herrscherclique 'regieren' zu lassen. Ist es nicht so, dass sich jeder ehrliche Deutsche heute seiner Regierung schämt, und wer von uns ahnt das Ausmaß der Schmach, die über uns und unsere Kinder kommen wird, wenn einst der Schleier von unseren Augen gefallen ist und die grauenvollsten und jegliches Maß unendlich überschreitenden Verbrechen ans Tageslicht treten? Wenn das deutsche Volk schon so in seinem tiefsten Wesen korrumpiert und zerfallen ist, dass es, ohne eine Hand zu regen, im leichtsinnigen Vertrauen auf eine fragwürdige Gesetzmäßigkeit der Geschichte das Höchste, das ein Mensch besitzt und das ihn über jede andere Kreatur erhöht, nämlich den freien Willen, preisgibt, die Freiheit des Menschen preisgibt, selbst mit einzugreifen in das Rad der Geschichte und es seiner vernünftigen Entscheidung unterzuordnen — wenn die Deutschen, so jeder Individualität bar, schon so sehr zur geistlosen und feigen Masse geworden sind, dann, ja dann verdienen sie den Untergang.

Pamphlets of the White Rose I

Complicity with the 'governance' of an irresponsible clique of rulers driven by their darkest urges, and complicity without resistance — nothing is more unworthy of a civilised people. Is it not so that in the present day, every honourable German is ashamed of their government? And who amongst us can foresee the extent of the infamy that will be on us, and on our children, when the veil is one day lifted from our eyes and the most horrific crimes, crimes beyond all measure, come to light? If, in their innermost being, the German people have been corrupted and degraded enough to betray the greatest quality humanity possesses, that quality which elevates them above all other creatures — free will — without so much as lifting a finger, foolishly trusting the dubious notion that history follows its natural course; if this people can betray the freedom[1] of humankind to intervene in the course of history and to subordinate it to its rational judgement; if the Germans, so utterly devoid of any kind of individuality, have already become such a weak and mindless horde: then yes, they truly deserve their own demise.

Goethe spricht von den Deutschen als einem tragischen Volke, gleich dem der Juden und Griechen, aber heute hat es eher den Anschein, als sei es eine seichte, willenlose Herde von Mitläufern, denen das Mark aus dem Innersten gesogen und die nun ihres Kerns beraubt, bereit sind, sich in den Untergang hetzen zu lassen. Es scheint so — aber es ist nicht so; vielmehr hat man in langsamer, trügerischer, systematischer Vergewaltigung jeden einzelnen in ein geistiges Gefängnis gesteckt, und erst als er darin gefesselt lag, wurde er sich des Verhängnisses bewusst. Wenige nur erkannten das drohende Verderben, und der Lohn für ihr heroisches Mahnen war der Tod. Über das Schicksal dieser Menschen wird noch zu reden sein.

Wenn jeder wartet, bis der andere anfängt, werden die Boten der rächenden Nemesis unaufhaltsam näher und näher rücken, dann wird auch das letzte Opfer sinnlos in den Rachen des unersättlichen Dämons geworfen sein. Daher muss jeder einzelne seiner Verantwortung als Mitglied der christlichen und abendländischen Kultur bewusst in dieser letzten Stunde sich wehren, soviel er kann, arbeiten wider die Geißel der Menschheit, wider den Faschismus und jedes ihm ähnliche System des absoluten Staates.

Goethe speaks of the Germans as a tragic people, much like the Jews or the Greeks, but these days, they seem more like a shallow, spineless herd of mindless followers[2] whose substance has been sucked out of them from within and who, robbed of their very core, allow themselves to be baited into their own demise. This seems like the truth, but it isn't; a slow, deceitful, systematic violation has locked every single one of us into a mental cage, and it is only once shackled that we become conscious of our fate. Very few recognised the impeding calamity, and the reward for their heroic warnings was death. Much remains to be said about the fate of these people.

If every one of us waits for someone else to start, then the heralds of avenging Nemesis will draw ever closer until the last sacrificial victim is vainly thrown into the jaws of a demon that will never be sated. Every individual must therefore fight back with an awareness of their responsibility as a member of Christian and Western culture, must work against the scourges of humanity, against fascism and all the systems of dictatorship that resemble it.

Leistet passiven Widerstand — W i d e r s t a n d —, wo immer
Ihr auch seid, verhindert das Weiterlaufen dieser atheistischen
Kriegsmaschine, ehe es zu spät ist, ehe die letzten Städte ein
Trümmerhaufen sind, gleich Köln, und ehe die letzte Jugend
des Volkes irgendwo für die Hybris eines Untermenschen
verblutet ist. Vergesst nicht, dass ein jedes Volk diejenige
Regierung verdient, die es erträgt!

Aus Friedrich Schiller, 'Die Gesetzgebung des Lykurgus und
Solon':

'.... Gegen seinen eigenen Zweck gehalten, ist die
Gesetzgebung des Lykurgus ein Meisterstück der Staats- und
Menschenkunde. Er wollte einen mächtigen, in sich selbst
gegründeten, unzerstörbaren Staat; politische Stärke und
Dauerhaftigkeit waren das Ziel, wonach er strebte, und dieses
Ziel hat er so weit erreicht, als unter seinen Umständen
möglich war. Aber hält man den Zweck, welchen Lykurgus
sich vorsetzte, gegen den Zweck der Menschheit, so muss eine
tiefe Missbilligung an die Stelle der Bewunderung treten, die
uns der erste flüchtige Blick abgewonnen hat. Alles darf dem
Besten des Staats zum Opfer gebracht werden, nur dasjenige
nicht, dem der Staat selbst nur als ein Mittel dient. Der Staat
selbst ist niemals Zweck, er ist nur wichtig als eine Bedingung,
unter welcher der Zweck der Menschheit erfüllt werden kann,
und dieser Zweck der Menschheit ist kein anderer, als
Ausbildung aller Kräfte des Menschen, Fortschreitung.

Wherever you may be, mount passive resistance —
RESISTANCE — obstruct the progress of this atheistic war
machine before it's too late, before, like Cologne, the last cities
are left in ruins, before the last remaining youths of this nation
bleed to death in some unknown place for the sake of the hubris
of a subhuman.[3] Remember that every people deserves the
government it is prepared to tolerate.

From Friedrich Schiller's *The Legislation of Lycurgus and Solon:*

'... Seen in the light of its chosen ends, Lycurgus' legislation is
a masterpiece of political and human science. He wanted a state
that was powerful, founded upon itself and indestructible; the
aims he set himself were political strength and longevity, and
he achieved these aims as far as was possible under the
circumstances he was facing. But if one confronts the aims of
Lycurgus with the aims of mankind, the admiration that a first
fleeting glance sparked in us must give way to deep
disapproval. One may sacrifice everything for the best of the
state, with one exception: that to which the state is only a
means. The state in and of itself is never the purpose; it is
merely the necessary condition under which the purpose of
mankind may be fulfilled — and this purpose is none other than
the development of a person's abilities to their full extent, that
is to say progress.

Hindert eine Staatsverfassung, dass alle Kräfte, die im Menschen liegen, sich entwickeln; hindert sie die Fortschreitung des Geistes, so ist sie verwerflich und schädlich, sie mag übrigens noch so durchdacht und in ihrer Art noch so vollkommen sein. Ihre Dauerhaftigkeit selbst gereicht ihr alsdann viel mehr zum Vorwurf als zum Ruhme — sie ist dann nur ein verlängertes Übel; je länger sie Bestand hat, um so schädlicher ist sie.

... Auf Unkosten aller sittlichen Gefühle wurde das politische Verdienst errungen und die Fähigkeit dazu ausgebildet. In Sparta gab es keine eheliche Liebe, keine Mutterliebe, keine kindliche Liebe, keine Freundschaft — es gab nichts als Bürger, nichts als bürgerliche Tugend.

... Ein Staatsgesetz machte den Spartanern die Unmenschlichkeit gegen ihre Sklaven zur Pflicht; in diesen unglücklichen Schlachtopfern wurde die Menschheit beschimpft und misshandelt.

In dem spartanischen Gesetzbuche selbst wurde der gefährliche Grundsatz gepredigt, Menschen als Mittel und nicht als Zwecke zu betrachten dadurch wurden die Grundfesten des Naturrechts und der Sittlichkeit gesetzmäßig eingerissen.

If a state's constitution hinders the development of all the inward powers of mankind, if it hinders the progress of the *Geist*,[4] then it is harmful and reprehensible, however well thought out and perfect a work of its kind it may be. And so its longevity comes to earn it more censure than glory, it becomes a prolonged curse; the longer it lasts, the more harmful it becomes.

... Political merit was achieved, and the ability to obtain it taught, at the extent of every moral sentiment. There was no marital love in Sparta, no mother's love, no child's love, no friendship; there were nothing but citizens, nothing but citizens' virtue.

... A state law made it a duty for Spartans to treat their slaves inhumanly; and in these wretched victims of butchery, humanity was violated and abused.

The Spartan Code of Law itself preached the dangerous principle that people were to be regarded as means and not ends, thereby constitutionally obliterating the foundations of natural law and morality.

... Welch schöneres Schauspiel gibt der rauhe Krieger Gaius Marcius in seinem Lager vor Rom, der Rache und Sieg aufopfert, weil er die Tränen der Mutter nicht fließen sehen kann!

... Der Staat (des Lykurgus) könnte nur unter der einzigen Bedingung fortdauern, wenn der Geist des Volks stillstünde; er könnte sich also nur dadurch erhalten, dass er den höchsten und einzigen Zweck eines Staates verfehlte.'

Aus Goethes 'Des Epimenides Erwachen', zweiter Aufzug, vierter Auftritt:

Genien
.....
Doch was dem Abgrund kühn entstiegen,
Kann durch ein ehernes Geschick
Den halben Weltkreis übersiegen,
Zum Abgrund muss es doch zurück.
Schon droht ein ungeheures Bangen,
Vergebens wird er widerstehn!
Und alle, die noch an ihm hangen,
Sie müssen mit zu Grunde gehn.

... There is no finer scene than that played out in his camp at the gates of Rome by the savage warrior Gaius Marcius who sacrificed revenge and victory because he could not bear to see his mother's tears!

... The state (of Lycurgus) could only subsist under one condition: the spirit of the nation would have to stand still; and to ensure its continued existence would therefore mean to neglect the highest and the sole aim of a state.'

From Goethe's *Epimenides Awakes*, Act II, scene 4:

Spirits

.....

What burst forth bold from the abyss
Could with a brazen mastery
Claim victory of half the globe —
Yet now back to the void it must.
A monstrous fear already looms,
And all resistance will be vain!
The ones who still cling on to it
Will perish with its name.

Hoffnung:

Nun begegn' ich meinen Braven,
Die sich in der Nacht versammelt,
Um zu schweigen, nicht zu schlafen,
Und das schöne Wort der Freiheit
Wird gelispelt und gestammelt,
Bis in ungewohnter Neuheit
Wir an unsrer Tempel Stufen
Wieder neu entzückt es rufen:
(Mit Überzeugung, laut:)
Freiheit!
(gemäßigter:)
Freiheit!
(von allen Seiten und Enden Echo:)
Freiheit!

Wir bitten Sie, dieses Blatt mit möglichst vielen Durchschlägen
abzuschreiben und weiterzuverteilen!

Hope:

And now I'll meet my brave of heart,
Who gather in the midst of night,
To share a silence, keep awake.
They stutter, stammer, on and on
That fair enchanting word: Freedom,
Till on our temple's steps anew
So youthful and so unfamiliar
We call its name, a joyful clamour:
(*With conviction, loud:*)
Freedom!
(*More moderately:*)
Freedom!
(*Echoing from all sides:*)
Freedom!

We urge you to transcribe this leaflet, make as many copies as you can and distribute them!

Notes

[1] 'Freiheit': 'freedom'. See the glossary for a discussion of this term.

[2] 'Mitläufer': 'fellow travellers'. See the glossary for a discussion of this term.

[3] 'Untermensch': 'subhuman'. This word was commonly used in Nazi propaganda to describe non-Aryan 'inferior people', including Jewish people, Roma, and Slavs, who were to be exterminated.

[4] 'Geist': German noun pertaining to philosophy. Its semantic field covers translations like 'spirit', 'mind', 'intellect', 'essence'. It is a central concept of German philosophy, especially in Hegel's *Phänomenologie des Geistes* (*The Phenomenology of Spirit*, 1807).

Translated by Louise Mayer-Jacquelin and Poppy Robertson.

THE SECOND PAMPHLET
Summer 1942

Flugblätter der Weissen Rose

II

Man kann sich mit dem Nationalsozialismus geistig nicht auseinandersetzen, weil er ungeistig ist. Es ist falsch, wenn man von einer nationalsozialistischen Weltanschauung spricht, denn, wenn es diese gäbe, müsste man versuchen, sie mit geistigen Mitteln zu beweisen oder zu bekämpfen - die Wirklichkeit aber bietet uns ein völlig anderes Bild: schon in ihrem ersten Keim war diese Bewegung auf den Betrug des Mitmenschen angewiesen, schon damals war sie im Innersten verfault und konnte sich nur durch die stete Lüge retten. Schreibt doch Hitler selbst in einer frühen Auflage "seines" Buches (ein Buch, das in dem übelsten Deutsch geschrieben worden ist, das ich je gelesen habe; dennoch ist es von dem Volke der Dichter und Denker zur Bibel erhoben worden): "Man glaubt nicht, wie man ein Volk betrügen muss, um es zu regieren." Wenn sich nun am Anfang dieses Krebsgeschwür des Deutschen Volkes noch nicht allzusehr bemerkbar gemacht hatte, so nur deshalb, weil noch gute Kräfte genug am Werk waren, es zurückzuhalten. Wie es aber grösser und grösser wurde und schliesslich mittels einer letzten gemeinen Korruption zur Macht kam, das Geschwür gleichsam aufbrach und den ganzen Körper besudelte, verstockte sich die Mehrzahl der früheren Gegner, flüchtete die deutsche Intelligenz in ein Kellerloch, um dort als Nachtschattengewächs, dem Licht und der Sonne verborgen, allmählich zu ersticken. Jetzt stehen wir vor dem Ende. Jetzt kommt es darauf an, sich gegenseitig wiederzufinden, aufzuklären von Mensch zu Mensch, immer daran zu denken und sich keine Ruhe zu geben, bis auch der letzte von der äussersten Notwendigkeit seines Kämpfens wider dieses System überzeugt ist. Wenn so eine Welle des Aufruhrs durch das Land geht, wenn "es in der Luft liegt", wenn viele mitmachen, dann kann in einer letzten, gewaltigen Anstrengung dieses System abgeschüttelt werden. Ein Ende mit Schrecken ist immer noch besser, als ein Schrecken ohne Ende.

Es ist uns nicht gegeben, ein endgültiges Urteil über den Sinn unserer Geschichte zu fällen. Aber wenn diese Katastrophe uns zum Heile dienen soll, so doch nur dadurch: Durch das Leid gereinigt zu werden, aus der tiefsten Nacht heraus das Licht zu ersehnen, sich aufzuraffen und endlich mitzuhelfen, das Joch abzuschütteln, das die Welt bedrückt.

Nicht über die Judenfrage wollen wir in diesem Blatte schreiben, keine Verteidigungsrede verfassen - nein, nur als Beispiel wollen wir die Tatsache kurz anführen, die Tatsache, dass seit der Eroberung Polens dreihunderttausend Juden in diesem Land auf bestialischste Art ermordet worden sind, Hier sehen wir das fürchterlichste Verbrechen an der Würde des Menschen, ein Verbrechen, dem sich kein ähnliches in der ganzen Menschengeschichte an die Seite stellen kann. Auch die Juden sind doch Menschen - man mag sich zur Judenfrage stellen wie man will - und an Menschen wurde solches verübt. Vielleicht sagt jemand, die Juden hätten ein solches Schicksal verdient; diese Behauptung wäre eine ungeheure Anmassung; aber angenommen, es sagte jemand dies, wie stellt er sich dann zu der Tatsache, dass die gesamte polnische adelige Jugend vernichtet worden ist (Gebe Gott, dass sie es noch nicht ist!) Auf welche Art, fragen sie, ist solches geschehen? Alle männlichen Sprösslinge aus adeligen Geschlechtern zwischen 15 und 20 Jahren wurden in Konzentrationslager nach Deutschland zu Zwangsarbeit, alle Mädchen gleichen Alters nach Norwegen in die Bordelle der SS verschleppt! Wozu wir dies Ihnen alles erzählen, da sie es schon selber wissen, wenn nicht diese, so andere gleich schwere Verbrechen des fürchterlichen Untermenschentums? Weil hier eine Frage berührt wird, die uns alle zutiefst angeht und allen zu denken geben muss: Warum verhält sich das deutsche

Volk angesichts all dieser schaudlichsten ,menschenunwürdigsten
Verbrechen so apathisch ? Kaum irgendjemand macht sich Gedanken darüber.
Die Tatsache wird als solche hingenommen und ad acta gelegt.Und wieder
schläft das deutsche Volk in seinen stumpfen,blöden Schlaf weiter und
gibt diesen faschistischenVerbrechern Mut und Gelegenheit weiterzuwüten -
und diese tun es. Sollte dies ein Zeichen dafür sein, dass die Deutschen
in ihren primitivsten menschlichen Gefühlen verroht sind, dass keine Saite
in ihnen schrill aufschreit im Angesicht solcher Taten, dass sie in einen
tödlichen Schlaf versunken sind,aus dem es kein Erwachen mehr gibt,nie,
niemals? Es scheint so und ist es bestimmt,wenn der Deutsche nicht endlich aus dieser Dumpfheit auffährt , wenn er nicht protestiert,wo immer
er nur kann gegen diese Verbrecherklique,wenn er mit diesen Hunderttausenden von Opfern nicht mitleidet .Und nicht nur Mitleid muss er empfinden,nein,noch viel mehr :M i t s c h u l d .Denn er gibt durch sein apa-
tisches Verhalten diesen dunklen Menschen erst die Möglichkeit so zu handeln,er leidet diese "Regierung",die eine so unendliche Schuld auf sich
geladen hat,ja er ist doch selbst schuld daran ,dass sie überhaupt entstehen konnte ! Ein jeder will sich von einer solchen Mitschuld freisprechen,ein jeder tut es und schläft dann wieder mit ruhigstem,bestem Gewis-
sen.Aber er kann sich nicht freisprechen,ein jeder ist s c h u l d i g ,
s c h u l d i g , s c h u l d i g ! Doch ist es noch nicht zu spät,diese
abscheulichste aller Missgeburten von Regierungen aus der Welt zu schaffen,um nicht noch mehr Schuld auf sich zu laden.Jetzt,da uns in den let-
ten Jahren die Augen vollkommen geöffnet worden sind,da wir wissen,mit wem
wir es zu tun haben,jetzt ist es allerhöchste Zeit,diese braune Horde
auszurotten.Bis zum Ausbruch des Krieges war der grösste Teil des deutsch-
en Volkes geblendet,die Nationalsozialisten zeigten sich nicht in ihrer
wahren Gestalt,doch jetzt,da man sie erkannt hat,muss es die einzige und
höchste Pflicht,ja heiligste Pflicht eines jeden Deutschen sein,diese
Bestien zu vertilgen !

"Der,des Verwaltung unauffällig ist,des
Volk ist froh.Der,des Verwaltung aufdringlich ist,des Volk ist gebrochen.
Elend ,ach,ist es,worauf Glück sich auf-
baut.Glück,ach,verschleiert nur Elend.Wo
soll das hinaus ? Des Ende ist nicht abzu-
sehen.Das Geordnete verkehrt sich in Unordnung,das Gute verkehrt sich in Schlechtes.
Das Volk gerät in Verwirrung.Ist es nicht
so täglich seit langem ?
Daher ist der Hohe Mensch rechteckig,aber
er stösst nicht an, er ist kantig, aber
verletzt nicht,er ist aufrecht,aber nicht
schroff.Er ist klar, aber will nicht
glänzen. "   Lao-tse.
. . . . .

Wer unternimmt, das Reich zu beherrschen,und es nach seiner
Willkür zu gestalten; ich sehe ihn sein Ziel nicht erreichen;
das ist alles.
Das Reich ist ein lebendiger Organismus; es kann nicht gemacht
werden, wahrlich! Wer daran machen will, verdirbt es,wer sich
seiner bemächtigen will,verliert es.
Daher: "Von den Wesen gehen manche voraus,andere folgen ihnen,
manche atmen warm,manche kalt,manche sind stark,manche schwach,
manche erlangen Fülle,andere unterliegen."
Der Hohe Mensch daher lässt ab von Uebertriebenheit,lässt ab
von Ueberhebung,lässt ab von Uebergriffen.   Lao-tse.
. . . . .
Wir bitten,dieses Schrift mit möglichst vielen Durchschlägen abzuschreiben und weiterzuverteilen.

Flugblätter der Weißen Rose II

Man kann sich mit dem Nationalsozialismus geistig nicht auseinandersetzen, weil er ungeistig ist. Es ist falsch, wenn man von einer nationalsozialistischen Weltanschauung spricht, denn wenn es diese gäbe, müsste man versuchen, sie mit geistigen Mitteln zu beweisen oder zu bekämpfen — die Wirklichkeit aber bietet uns ein völlig anderes Bild: schon in ihrem ersten Keim war diese Bewegung auf den Betrug des Mitmenschen angewiesen, schon damals war sie im Innersten verfault und konnte sich nur durch die stete Lüge retten. Schreibt doch Hitler selbst in einer frühen Auflage 'seines' Buches (ein Buch, das in dem übelsten Deutsch geschrieben worden ist, das ich je gelesen habe; dennoch ist es von dem Volke der Dichter und Denker zur Bibel erhoben worden): 'Man glaubt nicht, wie man ein Volk betrügen muss, um es zu regieren.' Wenn sich nun am Anfang dieses Krebsgeschwür des deutschen Volkes noch nicht allzusehr bemerkbar gemacht hatte, so nur deshalb, weil noch gute Kräfte genug am Werk waren, es zurückzuhalten. Wie es aber größer und größer wurde und schließlich mittels einer letzten gemeinen Korruption zur Macht kam, das Geschwür gleichsam aufbrach und den ganzen Körper besudelte, versteckte sich die Mehrzahl der früheren Gegner, flüchtete die deutsche Intelligenz in ein Kellerloch, um dort als Nachtschattengewächs, dem Licht und der Sonne verborgen, allmählich zu ersticken. Jetzt stehen wir vor dem Ende.

Pamphlets of the White Rose II

National Socialism cannot be confronted intellectually because it is not intellectual. It is wrong to speak of a National Socialist world view, because if such a thing existed, it would need to be proven or challenged by intellectual means — yet in reality we are presented with a completely different picture: even in its earliest embryonic form, this movement was dependent on deceiving the German people; even then, it was rotten to the very core and could only save itself through ceaseless deception. Even Hitler himself writes in an early edition of 'his' book (a book which, despite having been written in the most appalling German that I have ever read, has been elevated to biblical status by this nation of poets and philosophers): 'You would not believe the extent to which you must deceive a people in order to govern it.' If at first this cancerous tumour on the German people had not yet made itself all too conspicuous, this was only because there were still forces for good working effectively enough to hold it back. Yet as it became bigger and bigger and finally came to power with one last base act of corruption, the tumour, so to speak, ruptured, contaminating the whole body. The majority of its earlier opponents then went into hiding and the German intelligentsia sought refuge in a coal cellar only to gradually suffocate there, like nightshade hidden away from daylight and the sun. Now, we are approaching the end.

Jetzt kommt es darauf an, sich gegenseitig wiederzufinden, aufzuklären von Mensch zu Mensch, immer daran zu denken und sich keine Ruhe zu geben, bis auch der Letzte von der äußersten Notwendigkeit seines Kämpfens wider dieses System überzeugt ist. Wenn so eine Welle des Aufruhrs durch das Land geht, wenn 'es in der Luft liegt', wenn viele mitmachen, dann kann in einer letzten, gewaltigen Anstrengung dieses System abgeschüttelt werden. Ein Ende mit Schrecken ist immer noch besser als ein Schrecken ohne Ende.

Es ist uns nicht gegeben, ein endgültiges Urteil über den Sinn unserer Geschichte zu fällen. Aber wenn diese Katastrophe uns zum Heile dienen soll, so doch nur dadurch: durch das Leid gereinigt zu werden, aus der tiefsten Nacht heraus das Licht zu ersehnen, sich aufzuraffen und endlich mitzuhelfen, das Joch abzuschütteln, das die Welt bedrückt.

......

Nicht über die Judenfrage wollen wir in diesem Blatte schreiben, keine Verteidigungsrede verfassen — nein, nur als Beispiel wollen wir die Tatsache kurz anführen, die Tatsache, dass seit der Eroberung Polens <u>dreihunderttausend</u> Juden in diesem Land auf bestialischste Art ermordet worden sind. Hier sehen wir das fürchterlichste Verbrechen an der Würde des Menschen, ein Verbrechen, dem sich kein ähnliches in der ganzen Menschengeschichte an die Seite stellen kann.

Now, everything depends on finding one another again, on one person enlightening the next, always reflecting and never resting until every last person is convinced of the dire necessity of fighting against this system. If such a wave of uproar travels through the country, if there is 'something in the air', if many people get involved, then this system can be shaken off with one final tremendous effort. An end with terror is still better than terror without end.

It is not our place to give a final judgement on the meaning of our history. But if this catastrophe is to heal us, it will be solely by means of being purified by suffering, of yearning for the light in the very deepest darkness, by stirring ourselves, and finally, by playing our part in casting off the yoke which weighs down the world.

......

We do not want to write about the Jewish question in this pamphlet, nor to compose a plea of defence — no, we want only to briefly point out by way of example the fact that, since the conquest of Poland, three hundred thousand Jews have been murdered in that country in the most bestial manner. Here, we see the most horrific crime against human dignity, a crime unparalleled in all of human history.

Auch die Juden sind doch Menschen — man mag sich zur Judenfrage stellen wie man will —, und an Menschen wurde solches verübt. Vielleicht sagt jemand, die Juden hätten ein solches Schicksal verdient; diese Behauptung wäre eine ungeheure Anmaßung; aber angenommen, es sagte jemand dies, wie stellt er sich dann zu der Tatsache, dass die gesamte polnische adelige Jugend vernichtet worden ist (gebe Gott, dass sie es noch nicht ist!)? Auf welche Art, fragen Sie, ist solches geschehen? Alle männlichen Sprösslinge aus adeligen Geschlechtern zwischen 15 und 20 Jahren wurden in Konzentrationslager nach Deutschland zur Zwangsarbeit, alle Mädchen gleichen Alters nach Norwegen in die Bordelle der SS verschleppt! Wozu wir dies Ihnen alles erzählen, da Sie es schon selber wissen, wenn nicht diese, so andere gleich schwere Verbrechen des fürchterlichen Untermenschentums? Weil hier eine Frage berührt wird, die uns alle zutiefst angeht und allen zu denken geben   m u s s . Warum verhält sich das deutsche Volk   angesichts   all   dieser   scheußlichsten menschenunwürdigsten Verbrechen so apathisch? Kaum irgend jemand macht sich Gedanken darüber. Die Tatsache wird als solche hingenommen und ad acta gelegt. Und wieder schläft das deutsche Volk in seinem stumpfen, blöden Schlaf weiter und gibt diesen faschistischen Verbrechern Mut und Gelegenheit, weiterzutöten —, und diese tun es.

For Jews are human beings too — whichever stance one might take on the Jewish question — and it is against human beings that this has been committed. Some might say that the Jews deserved such a fate; this would be a claim of colossal arrogance — but, assuming that someone did say this, what stance would they then take towards the fact that the entire youth of Poland's aristocracy has been annihilated (God grant that this is not yet the case!)? How, you ask, has such a thing occurred? All the male offspring of aristocratic families between the ages of 15 and 20 were carted off to Germany for forced labour in the concentration camps, and all the girls of the same age to Norway into the brothels of the SS! Why are we telling you all this, given that you already know about it, or if not about this, then about other, equally serious crimes of this appalling sub-humanity? Because it touches on an issue that deeply concerns us all and MUST give us pause for thought. Why do the German people[1] behave so apathetically in the face of all these most atrocious, most inhumane crimes? Barely anyone gives it a thought. The fact is accepted as such and filed away. And again, the German people return to their dull, stupid sleep and give these fascist criminals the courage and the opportunity to go on rampaging —, and that is precisely what they do.

Sollte dies ein Zeichen dafür sein, dass die Deutschen in ihren primitivsten menschlichen Gefühlen verroht sind, dass keine Saite in ihnen schrill aufschreit im Angesicht solcher Taten, dass sie in einen tödlichen Schlaf versunken sind, aus dem es kein Erwachen mehr gibt, nie, niemals? Es scheint so und ist es bestimmt, wenn der Deutsche nicht endlich aus dieser Dumpfheit auffährt, wenn er nicht protestiert, wo immer er nur kann, gegen diese Verbrecherclique, wenn er mit diesen Hunderttausenden von Opfern nicht mitleidet. Und nicht nur Mitleid muss er empfinden, nein, noch viel mehr: M i t s c h u l d . Denn er gibt durch sein apathisches Verhalten diesen dunklen Menschen erst die Möglichkeit, so zu handeln, er leidet diese 'Regierung', die eine so unendliche Schuld auf sich geladen hat, ja, er ist doch selbst schuld daran, dass sie überhaupt entstehen konnte! Ein jeder will sich von einer solchen Mitschuld freisprechen, ein jeder tut es und schläft dann wieder mit ruhigstem, bestem Gewissen. Aber er kann sich nicht freisprechen, ein jeder ist s c h u l d i g , s c h u l d i g , s c h u l d i g ! Doch ist es noch nicht zu spät, diese abscheulichste aller Missgeburten von Regierungen aus der Welt zu schaffen, um nicht noch mehr Schuld auf sich zu laden.

Should this be taken as a sign that the Germans' most primitive, human emotions have been rendered so brutal that no voice within them cries out piercingly in the face of such deeds, that they have sunk into a deadly sleep, from which there is no awakening, not ever? This is how it seems, and it certainly will be, if Germany does not start up from this apathy, if she does not protest against this clique of criminals wherever she can, if she does not feel a collective suffering with these hundreds of thousands of victims. And she must not only feel collective suffering, no, much more: COLLECTIVE GUILT.[2] Since, through her apathetic behaviour, she gives these dark leaders the opportunity to act this way in the first place, she suffers this 'government', which has burdened itself with such endless guilt; yet it is her own fault that it was able to emerge in the first place! Everyone wants to exonerate themselves from such a collective guilt, everyone does so and returns to sleeping soundly with the calmest, clearest conscience. But no one can exonerate themselves, everyone is GUILTY, GUILTY, GUILTY! Yet it is not too late to rid the world of this most heinous monstrosity of a government, so we do not further yoke ourselves to guilt.

Jetzt, da uns in den letzten Jahren die Augen vollkommen geöffnet worden sind, da wir wissen, mit wem wir es zu tun haben, jetzt ist es allerhöchste Zeit, diese braune Horde auszurotten. Bis zum Ausbruch des Krieges war der größte Teil des deutschen Volkes geblendet, die Nationalsozialisten zeigten sich nicht in ihrer wahren Gestalt, doch jetzt, da man sie erkannt hat, muss es die einzige und höchste Pflicht, ja heiligste Pflicht eines jeden Deutschen sein, diese Bestien zu vertilgen.

'Der, des Verwaltung unauffällig ist, des Volk ist froh. Der, des Verwaltung aufdringlich ist, des Volk ist gebrochen. Elend, ach, ist es, worauf Glück sich aufbaut. Glück, ach, verschleiert nur Elend. Wo soll das hinaus? Das Ende ist nicht abzusehen. Das Geordnete verkehrt sich in Unordnung, das Gute verkehrt sich in Schlechtes. Das Volk gerät in Verwirrung. Ist es nicht so, täglich, seit langem? Daher ist der Hohe Mensch rechteckig, aber er stößt nicht an, er ist kantig, aber verletzt nicht, er ist aufrecht, aber nicht schroff. Er ist klar, aber will nicht glänzen.' Lao-tse.

'Wer unternimmt, das Reich zu beherrschen und es nach seiner Willkür zu gestalten; ich sehe ihn sein Ziel nicht erreichen; das ist alles.'

Now, since our eyes have been fully opened over the last few years, since we know whom we're dealing with, it is high time to exterminate this brown-shirt horde. Until the outbreak of the war, the vast majority of the German people were blinded, the National Socialists did not show their true face, but now, since they have been seen for what they are, the highest and only duty, the most sacred duty even of every German must be to destroy these beasts.

'If a regime is unobtrusive, its people are happy. If a regime is oppressive, the people are broken. Misery, alas, is what happiness is built upon. Happiness, alas, only veils misery. Where does all this lead? The end is nowhere in sight. Order lapses into disorder, good lapses into evil. The people fall into disarray. Has this not long been the case, day in, day out? Therefore, the wise man is angular, but does not scrape; he has edges, but does not hurt anyone; he stands strong, but without being harsh. He is bright, but he does not wish to gleam.' Laozi.

'He who sets out to rule over the empire[3] and to shape it as he pleases; I do not see him achieving his aim; that is all.'

'Das Reich ist ein lebendiger Organismus; es kann nicht gemacht werden, wahrlich! Wer daran machen will, verdirbt es, wer sich seiner bemächtigen will, verliert es.'

Daher: 'Von den Wesen gehen manche vorauf, andere folgen ihnen, manche atmen warm, manche kalt, manche sind stark, manche schwach, manche erlangen Fülle, andere unterliegen.'

'Der Hohe Mensch daher lässt ab von Übertriebenheit, lässt ab von Überhebung, lässt ab von Übergriffen.' Lao-tse.

·········

Wir bitten, diese Schrift mit möglichst vielen Durchschlägen abzuschreiben und weiterzuverteilen.

'The empire is a living organism; in truth, it cannot be constructed!' He who seeks to construct it, corrupts it, he who seeks to grasp it, loses it.'

Therefore: 'Some beings go on ahead, others follow them, some have warm breath, others cold, some are strong, others weak, some reach fulfilment, others are overcome.'

'The wise man therefore refrains from exaggeration, from extremes, and from excess.' Laozi.

. . . .

Please copy this document and distribute it as widely as possible.

Notes

[1] 'Volk': 'people', 'nation'. See the glossary for a discussion of this term.

[2] 'Mitschuld': 'collective responsibility'. See the glossary. 'Mitleid' really means 'compassion', which though it has etymologically the sense of 'suffering with' has shifted meaning over time. Here, the translation attempts to reflect the wordplay in the German original.

[3] It is worth noting here that the German translation of Laozi's aphorism which the White Rose have used includes the word 'Reich' which we have translated as 'empire'. This Laozi quotation therefore acquires greater significance, since it implies a connection with the National Socialist regime, which was officially known as the 'Drittes Reich' ('Third Reich'). This title designates Hitler's dictatorship as the third German empire after the Holy Roman Empire (800-1806) and the German Empire (1871-1918).

Translated by Pauline Gümpel, Eve Mason, and Timothy Powell.

THE THIRD PAMPHLET
Summer 1942

Flugblätter der Weissen Rose

III

"Salus publica suprema lex."

Alle idealen Staatsformen sind Utopien. Ein Staat kann nicht rein theoretisch konstruiert werden, sondern er muss ebenso wachsen, reifen, wie der einzelne Mensch. Aber es ist nicht zu vergessen, dass am Anfang einer jeden Kultur die Vorform des Staates vorhanden war. Die Familie ist so alt, wie die Menschen selbst und aus diesem anfänglichen Zusammensein hat sich der vernunftbegabte Mensch einen Staat geschaffen, dessen Grund die Gerechtigkeit und dessen höchstes Gesetz das Wohl Aller sein soll. Der Staat soll eine Analogie der göttlichen Ordnung darstellen, und die höchste aller Utopien, die civitas Dei ist das Vorbild, dem er sich letzten Endes nähern soll. Wir wollen hier nicht urteilen über die verschiedenen möglichen Staatsformen, die Demokratie, die konstitutionelle Monarchie, das Königtum usw. Nur eines will eindeutig und klar herausgehoben werden: jeder einzelne Mensch hat einen Anspruch auf einen brauchbaren und gerechten Staat, der die Freiheit des Einzelnen als auch das Wohl der Gesamtheit, sichert. Denn der Mensch soll nach Gottes Willen frei und unabhängig im Zusammenleben und Zusammenwirken der staatlichen Gemeinschaft sein natürliches Ziel, sein irdisches Glück in Selbstständigkeit und Selbsttätigkeit zu erreichen suchen.

Unser heutiger "Staat" aber ist die Diktatur des Bösen. "Das wissen wir schon lange," höre ich Dich einwenden, "und wir haben es nicht nötig, dass uns dies hier noch einmal vorgehalten wird." Aber, frage ich Dich, wenn ihr das wisst, warum regt ihr euch nicht, warum duldet ihr, dass diese Gewalthaber Schritt für Schritt offen und im Verborgenen eine Domäne eures Rechtes nach der anderen rauben, bis eines Tages nichts, aber auch gar nichts Übrigbleiben wird, als ein mechanisiertes Staatsgetriebe, kommandiert von Verbrechern und Säufern? Ist euer Geist schon so sehr der Vergewaltigung unterlegen, dass ihr vergesst, dass es nicht nur euer Recht, sondern eure s i t t l i c h e P f l i c h t ist, dieses System zu beseitigen? Wenn aber ein Mensch nicht mehr die Kraft aufbringt, sein Recht zu fordern, dann muss er mit absoluter Notwendigkeit untergehen. Wir würden es verdienen, in alle Welt verstreut zu werden, wie der Staub vor dem Winde, wenn wir uns in dieser zwölften Stunde nicht aufrafften und endlich den Mut aufbrächten, der uns seither gefehlt hat. Verbergt nicht eure Feigheit unter dem Mantel der Klugheit! Denn mit jedem Tag, da ihr noch zögert, da ihr dieser Ausgeburt der Hölle nicht widersteht, wächst eure Schuld gleich einer parabolischen Kurve höher und immer höher.

Viele, vielleicht die meisten Leser dieser Blätter sind sich darüber nicht klar, wie sie einen Widerstand ausüben sollen. Sie sehen keine Möglichkeiten. Wir wollen versuchen Ihnen zu zeigen, dass ein jeder in der Lage ist, etwas beizutragen zum Sturz dieses Systems. Nicht durch individualistische Gegnerschaft, in der Art verbitterter Einsiedler, wird es möglich werden, den Boden für einen Sturz dieser "Regierung" reif zu machen oder gar den Umsturz möglichst bald herbeizuführen, sondern nur durch die Zusammenarbeit vieler überzeugter, tatkräftiger Menschen, Menschen, die sich einig sind, mit welchen Mitteln sie ihr Ziel erreichen können. Wir haben keine reiche Auswahl an solchen Mitteln, nur ein einziges steht uns zur Verfügung - der p a s s i v e W i d e r s t a n d .

Der Sinn und das Ziel des passiven Widerstandes ist,den Nationalsozialismus zu Fall zu bringen und in diesem Kampf ist vor keinem Weg,
vor keiner Tat zurückzuschrecken,mögen sie auf Gebieten liegen,auf welchen sie auch wollen.An a l l e n Stellen muss der Nationalsozialismus
angegriffen werden, an denen er nur angreifbar ist.Ein Ende muss diesem
Unstaat möglichst bald bereitet werden - ein Sieg des faschistischen Deutschland in diesem Kriege hätte unabsehbare,fürchterliche Folgen.Nicht der
militärische Sieg über den Bolschewismus darf die erste Sorge für jeden
Deutschen sein,sondern die Niederlage der Nationalsozialisten.Dies muss
unbedingt an erster Stelle stehn.Die grössere Notwendigkeit dieser letz-
teren Forderung werden wir Ihnen in einem unserer nächsten Blätter beweisen.

Und jetzt muss sich ein jeder entschiedene Gegner des Nationalsozialismus die Frage vorlegen : Wie kann er gegen den gegenwärtigen "Staat"
am wirksamsten ankämpfen,wie ihm die empfindlichsten Schläge beibringen?
Durch den passiven Widerstand - zweifellos. Es ist klar, dass wir unmöglich für jeden Einzelnen Richtlinien für sein Verhalten geben können,nur
allgemein andeuten können wir,den Weg zur Verwirklichung muss Jeder selber
finden.

S a b o t a g e in Rüstungs - und kriegswichtigen Betrieben,Sabotage
in allen Versammlungen,Kundgebungen,Feetlichkeiten,Organisationen,die durch
die nat.soz.Partei ins Leben gerufen werden.Verhinderung des reibungslosen
Ablaufs der Kriegsmaschine (einer Maschine,die nur für einen Krieg arbeitet,der a l l e i n um die Rettung und Erhaltung der nat.soz.Partei und
ihrer Diktatur geht).S a b o t a g e auf allen wissenschaftlichen und
geistigen Gebieten,die für eine Fortführung des gegenwärtigen Krieges tätig sind- sei es in Universitäten,Hochschulen,Laboratorien,Forschungsan-
stalten,technischen Büros.S a b o t a g e in allen Veranstaltungen kultureller Art,die das "Ansehen" der Faschisten im Volke heben könnten.S a b o -
t a g e in allen Zweigen der bildenden Künste,die nur im geringsten im
Zusammenhang mit dem Nationalsozialismus stehen und ihm dienen.S a b o t a
g e in allem Schrifttum,allen Zeitungen,die im Solde der "Regierung" steh-
en,für ihre Ideen,für die Verbreitung der braunen Lüge,kämpfen.Opfert nicht
einen Pfennig bei Strassensammlungen (auch wenn sie unter dem Deckmantel
wohltätiger Zwecke durchgeführt werden.Denn dies ist nur eine Tarnung.In
Wirklichkeit kommt das Ergebnis weder dem Roten Kreuz noch den Notleidenden zugute.Die Regierung braucht dies Geld nicht,ist auf diese Sammlungen
finanziell nicht angewiesen - die Druckmaschinen laufen ja ununterbrochen
und stellen jede beliebige Menge von Papiergeld her.Das Volk muss aber d-
ernd in Spannung gehalten werden,nie darf der Druck der Kandare nachlass.
Gebt nichts für die Metall- Spinnstoff- und andere Sammlungen!Sucht alle
Bekannte auch aus den unteren Volksschichten,von der Sinnlosigkeit einer
Fortführung,von der Aussichtslosigkeit dieses Krieges,von der geistigen
und wirtschaftlichen Versklavung durch den Nationalsozialismus,von der
Zerstörung aller sittlichen und religiösen Werte zu überzeugen und zum
p a s s i v e n W i d e r s t a n d zu veranlassen!

- - - - - - - - - - - - - - -

Aristoteles "Über die Politik" : ....."Ferner gehört es (zum
Wesen der Tyrannis) dahin zu streben, dass ja nichts verborgen bleibe,
was irgend ein Untertan spricht oder tut, sondern überall Späher ihn belauschen ....ferner alle Welt miteinander zu verhetzen und Freunde mit
Freunden zu verfeinden und das Volk mit den Vornehmen und die Reichen
unter sich. Sodann gehört es zu solchen tyrannischen Massregeln, die
Untertanen arm zu machen, damit die Leibwache besoldet werden kann, und
sie, mit der Sorge um ihren täglichen Erwerb beschäftigt, keine Zeit und
Musse haben, Verschwörungen anzustiften....Ferner aber auch solche hohe
Einkommensteuern, wie die in Syrakus auferlegten, denn unter Dionysios
hatten die Bürger dieses Staates in fünf Jahren glücklich ihr ganzes Ver-
mögen in Steuern ausgegeben. Und auch beständig Kriege zu erregen ist der
Tyrann geneigt..."
Bitte vervielfältigen und weitergeben!!!

Flugblätter der Weißen Rose III

'Salus publica suprema lex.'

Alle idealen Staatsformen sind Utopien. Ein Staat kann nicht rein theoretisch konstruiert werden, sondern er muss ebenso wachsen, reifen wie der einzelne Mensch. Aber es ist nicht zu vergessen, dass am Anfang einer jeden Kultur die Vorform des Staates vorhanden war. Die Familie ist so alt wie die Menschen selbst, und aus diesem anfänglichen Zusammensein hat sich der vernunftbegabte Mensch einen Staat geschaffen, dessen Grund die Gerechtigkeit und dessen höchstes Gesetz das Wohl Aller sein soll. Der Staat soll eine Analogie der göttlichen Ordnung darstellen, und die höchste aller Utopien, die civitas Dei, ist das Vorbild, dem er sich letzten Endes nähern soll. Wir wollen hier nicht urteilen über die verschiedenen möglichen Staatsformen, die Demokratie, die konstitutionelle Monarchie, das Königtum usw. Nur eines will eindeutig und klar herausgehoben werden: jeder einzelne Mensch hat einen Anspruch auf einen brauchbaren und gerechten Staat, der die Freiheit des einzelnen als auch das Wohl der Gesamtheit sichert.

Pamphlets of the White Rose III

'Salus publica suprema lex.'[1]

All ideal forms of state are utopias. A state cannot be constructed in purely theoretical terms, but must grow and mature in the same way as every individual person. But we must not forget that an early form of the state was present at the beginning of every culture. The family is as old as humanity itself and from this original unit people, endowed with reason, created a state whose foundation was to be justice and whose supreme law was to be the common good. The state should be analogous to the divine order, and the greatest of all utopias, the Civitas Dei,[2] is the ideal that it should ultimately resemble. We do not want to pass judgement here on the various possible forms of state: democracy, constitutional or absolute monarchy, etc. Only one thing must be made unambiguously clear: every single person is entitled to a viable and just government that ensures the freedom[3] of the individual as well as the welfare of society as a whole.

Denn der Mensch soll nach Gottes Willen frei und unabhängig im Zusammenleben und Zusammenwirken der staatlichen Gemeinschaft sein natürliches Ziel, sein irdisches Glück in Selbständigkeit und Selbsttätigkeit zu erreichen suchen.

Unser heutiger 'Staat' aber ist die Diktatur des Bösen. 'Das wissen wir schon lange,' höre ich Dich einwenden, 'und wir haben es nicht nötig, dass uns dies hier noch einmal vorgehalten wird.' Aber, frage ich Dich, wenn Ihr das wisst, warum regt Ihr Euch nicht, warum duldet Ihr, dass diese Gewalthaber Schritt für Schritt offen und im verborgenen eine Domäne Eures Rechts nach der anderen rauben, bis eines Tages nichts, aber auch gar nichts übrigbleiben wird als ein mechanisiertes Staatsgetriebe, kommandiert von Verbrechern und Säufern? Ist Euer Geist schon so sehr der Vergewaltigung unterlegen, dass Ihr vergesst, dass es nicht nur euer Recht, sondern eure s i t t l i c h e P f l i c h t ist, dieses System zu beseitigen? Wenn aber ein Mensch nicht mehr die Kraft aufbringt, sein Recht zu fordern, dann muss er mit absoluter Notwendigkeit untergehen. Wir würden es verdienen, in alle Welt verstreut zu werden wie der Staub vor dem Winde, wenn wir uns in dieser zwölften Stunde nicht aufrafften und endlich den Mut aufbrächten, der uns seither gefehlt hat. Verbergt nicht Eure Feigheit unter dem Mantel der Klugheit.

For each person should, in accordance with God's will, freely and independently seek to achieve their natural goal, that is their earthly happiness through self-reliance and initiative, while co-existing and co-operating within the state as a community.

But our current 'state' is the dictatorship of evil. 'We know that already,' I hear you object, 'and we don't need you to reproach us for it yet again.' But, I ask you, if you know that, then why don't you act? Why do you tolerate these rulers gradually robbing you, in public and in private, of one right after another, until one day nothing, absolutely nothing, remains but the machinery of the state, under the command of criminals and drunkards? Has this violation defeated your spirit to such an extent that you have forgotten that it is not only your right but also your MORAL DUTY to do away with this system? But if a person can no longer summon the strength to demand their rights, they will certainly perish. We deserve to be scattered across the world like dust before the wind if we do not prepare ourselves for action now, at the eleventh hour, and finally muster the courage which we have thus far lacked. Do not conceal your cowardice under the cloak of expediency.

Denn mit jedem Tag, da Ihr noch zögert, da Ihr dieser Ausgeburt der Hölle nicht widersteht, wächst Eure Schuld gleich einer parabolischen Kurve höher und immer höher.

Viele, vielleicht die meisten Leser dieser Blätter sind sich darüber nicht klar, wie sie einen Widerstand ausüben sollen. Sie sehen keine Möglichkeiten. Wir wollen versuchen, ihnen zu zeigen, dass ein jeder in der Lage ist, etwas beizutragen zum Sturz dieses Systems. Nicht durch individualistische Gegnerschaft, in der Art verbitterter Einsiedler, wird es möglich werden, den Boden für einen Sturz dieser 'Regierung' reif zu machen oder gar den Umsturz möglichst bald herbeizuführen, sondern nur durch die Zusammenarbeit vieler überzeugter, tatkräftiger Menschen, Menschen, die sich einig sind, mit welchen Mitteln sie ihr Ziel erreichen können. Wir haben keine reiche Auswahl an solchen Mitteln, nur ein einziges steht uns zur Verfügung — der p a s s i v e W i d e r s t a n d.

Der Sinn und das Ziel des passiven Widerstandes ist, den Nationalsozialismus zu Fall zu bringen, und in diesem Kampf ist vor keinem Weg, vor keiner Tat zurückzuschrecken, mögen sie auf Gebieten liegen, auf welchen sie auch wollen. An allen Stellen muss der Nationalsozialismus angegriffen werden, an denen er nur angreifbar ist.

For with every day that you continue to hesitate, that you do not resist this spawn of hell, your guilt grows exponentially greater.[4]

Many, perhaps even the majority, of those reading these leaflets have no idea how they should mount resistance. They cannot see how it is possible. We aim to show them that each and every one of them is in a position to contribute to the overthrow of this system. It will not be possible to lay the foundations for the swift downfall of this 'government' or even to bring about its downfall through individualistic opposition like an embittered hermit; it is only through the conviction and energy of people acting together, people who are agreed on the means that can be used to achieve their goal. We do not have a vast range of means at our disposal, we have only one: PASSIVE RESISTANCE.

The meaning and purpose of passive resistance is to bring down National Socialism and, in this struggle, there is no course, no action that we should fear to take, whatever it may be. National Socialism must be attacked at every weak point, at every chink in its armour.

Ein Ende mus diesem Unstaat möglichst bald bereitet werden — ein Sieg des faschistischen Deutschland in diesem Kriege hätte unabsehbare, fürchterliche Folgen. Nicht der militärische Sieg über den Bolschewismus darf die erste Sorge für jeden Deutschen sein, sondern die Niederlage der Nationalsozialisten. Dies muss <u>unbedingt</u> an erster Stelle stehen. Die größere Notwendigkeit dieser letzten Forderung werden wir Ihnen in einem unserer nächsten Blätter beweisen.

Und jetzt muss sich ein jeder entschiedene Gegner des Nationalsozialismus die Frage vorlegen: Wie kann er gegen den gegenwärtigen 'Staat' am wirksamsten ankämpfen, wie ihm die empfindlichsten Schläge beibringen? Durch den passiven Widerstand — zweifellos. Es ist klar, dass wir unmöglich für jeden einzelnen Richtlinien für sein Verhalten geben können, nur allgemein andeuten können wir, den Weg zur Verwirklichung muss jeder selber finden.

S a b o t a g e in Rüstungs- und kriegswichtigen Betrieben, Sabotage in allen Versammlungen, Kundgebungen, Festlichkeiten, Organisationen, die durch die nat. soz. Partei ins Leben gerufen werden. Verhinderung des reibungslosen Ablaufs der Kriegsmaschine (einer Maschine, die nur für einen Krieg arbeitet, der allein um die Rettung und Erhaltung der nationalsozialistischen Partei und ihrer Diktatur geht).

This false state[5] must be brought to an end as soon as possible
— in this war, a victory for fascist Germany would have
dreadful, unimaginable consequences. The Germans' most
immediate concern should not be military victory over
Bolshevism, but defeating the National Socialists. This <u>must</u> be
our most urgent priority. We will illustrate how pressing this
is in one of our next pamphlets.

And now, every staunch adversary of National
Socialism must ask themselves the question: how can they fight
back against the current 'government' most effectively, how
can they inflict the most stinging wounds? The answer is,
without a doubt: passive resistance. It is clearly impossible for
us to provide every individual with direct instructions, we can
only give general suggestions, each person must find their own
way to put them into practice.

SABOTAGE of arms factories and other strategic
operations, sabotage of all conferences, rallies, festivities,
organizations, everything that the National Socialist Party
brought into being. Any and all hindrance to the smooth
operation of the war machine (a machine that is engineered
only for war, a war with the sole purpose of saving and
preserving the National Socialist Party and its dictatorship).

S a b o t a g e auf allen wissenschaftlichen und geistigen Gebieten, die für eine Fortführung des gegenwärtigen Krieges tätig sind — sei es in Universitäten, Hochschulen, Laboratorien, Forschungsanstalten, technischen Büros. S a b o t a g e in allen Veranstaltungen kultureller Art, die das 'Ansehen' der Faschisten im Volke heben könnten. S a b o t a g e in allen Zweigen der bildenden Künste, die nur im geringsten im Zusammenhang mit dem Nationalsozialismus stehen und ihm dienen. S a b o t a g e in allem Schrifttum, allen Zeitungen, die im Solde der 'Regierung' stehen, für ihre Ideen, für die Verbreitung der braunen Lüge kämpfen. Opfert nicht einen Pfennig bei Straßensammlungen (auch wenn sie unter dem Deckmantel wohltätiger Zwecke durchgeführt werden). Denn dies ist nur eine Tarnung. In Wirklichkeit kommt das Ergebnis weder dem Roten Kreuz noch den Notleidenden zugute. Die Regierung braucht dies Geld nicht, ist auf diese Sammlungen finanziell nicht angewiesen — die Druckmaschinen laufen ja ununterbrochen und stellen jede beliebige Menge Papiergeld her. Das Volk muss aber dauernd in Spannung gehalten werden, nie darf der Druck der Kandare nachlassen! Gebt nichts für die Metall-, Spinnstoff- und andere Sammlungen.

SABOTAGE of all academic and intellectual groups that actively support the continuation of the War — whether they are universities, colleges, laboratories, research institutes, or technical firms. SABOTAGE of all cultural events that might raise the fascists' 'prestige' with the people.[6] SABOTAGE of all branches of the arts that have the slightest connection to National Socialism or stand in its service. SABOTAGE of all publications, all newspapers that are in the pay of the 'government', that propagate its ideas and the spread the brown lie.[7] Do not give a single penny to street collections (even if they are carried out under the pretence of a charitable cause). This is only a cover. In reality, the sum will not benefit the Red Cross, or the needy. The government does not need this money, it is not financially dependent on these collections — their printing presses are running day and night, and can produce all the money they need. But they have to keep the people in a state of tension, held on a tight rein that must never be loosened! Do not donate any scrap metal, any fabric, or anything else!

Sucht alle Bekannten auch aus den unteren Volksschichten von der Sinnlosigkeit einer Fortführung, von der Aussichtslosigkeit dieses Krieges, von der geistigen und wirtschaftlichen Versklavung durch den Nationalsozialismus, von der Zerstörung aller sittlichen und religiösen Werte zu überzeugen und zum p a s s i v e n W i d e r s t a n d zu veranlassen!

Aristoteles, 'Über die Politik': '... ferner gehört es' (zum Wesen der Tyrannis), 'dahin zu streben, dass ja nichts verborgen bleibe, was irgendein Untertan spricht oder tut, sondern überall Späher ihn belauschen, ... ferner alle Welt miteinander zu verhetzen und Freunde mit Freunden zu verfeinden und das Volk mit den Vornehmen und die Reichen unter sich. Sodann gehört es zu solchen tyrannischen Maßregeln, die Untertanen arm zu machen, damit die Leibwache besoldet werden kann, und sie, mit der Sorge um ihren täglichen Erwerb beschäftigt, keine Zeit und Muße haben, Verschwörungen anzustiften... Ferner aber auch solche hohe Einkommensteuern, wie die in Syrakus auferlegten, denn unter Dionysios hatten die Bürger dieses Staates in fünf Jahren glücklich ihr ganzes Vermögen in Steuern ausgegeben. Und auch beständig Kriege zu erregen, ist der Tyrann geneigt...'

Bitte vervielfältigen und weitergeben!!!

Do your utmost to convince all your acquaintances, from the lower classes too, of the senselessness and futility of continuing this war, of the spiritual and economic enslavement, of the destruction of all moral and religious values, which has been brought about by National Socialism, and to encourage PASSIVE RESISTANCE!

Aristotle's *Politics*: '... a further essential aspect (of tyranny) is seeking to ensure that nothing any subject says or does remains hidden, but rather to spy and eavesdrop on him at every turn... and moreover to fill the whole world with hatred and to turn friend against friend, the people against the aristocracy, and the wealthy against one another. Thus an aspect of tyrannical discipline is making the subjects poor, so that the guards can be paid and so that they are so concerned about their daily earnings that they have no time or energy to to plot a coup-d'état'... Another aspect of tyranny is the implementation of high income taxes, such as were imposed on Syracuse, for after five years under Dionysius's rule the citizens had happily given up all their wealth in taxes. And the tyrant also has a constant inclination to provoke war...'

Please reproduce this and pass it on!!!

Notes

[1] 'The welfare of the people [is the] supreme law.' This is a misquotation of Cicero, *De Legibus* (book 3, part 3, sub. VIII), 'Salus populi suprema lex esto'.

[2] A reference to Saint Augustine of Hippo's *De civitas Dei contra paganos* (*The City of God against the Pagans*, c. 1470).

[3] Freiheit': 'freedom'. See the glossary for a discussion of this term.

[4] The German makes direct reference to a parabolic curve ('gleich einer parabolischen Kurve') where any point is at an equal distance from a fixed point and a fixed straight line. For a discussion of our approach to translating this phrase, see p. 104.

[5] Here the word 'Unstaat' is used. For a discussion of the words 'Staat' and 'Unstaat', see the glossary.

[6] 'Volk': 'people', 'nation'. See the glossary.

[7] The colour brown had been associated with the Nazis since the 1920s, when Hitler's Munich-based militia, the 'Sturmabteilung' ('Storm Detachment'), wore brown shirts as their uniform. Even after much of the 'Sturmabteilung' was purged by the SS in the 'Night of the Long Knives' in June 1934, the use of the word 'brown' as a shorthand for 'Nazi' or 'fascist' persisted.

Translated by Zoë Aebischer, Harry Smith,
and Madeleine Williamson-Sarll.

THE FOURTH PAMPHLET

Summer 1942

F l u g b l ä t t e r   d e r   W e i s s e n   R o s e

IV

Es ist eine alte Weisheit, die man Kindern immer wieder aufs
neue predigt, dass wer nicht hören will, fühlen muss. Ein kluges Kind
wird sich aber die Finger nur einmal am heissen Ofen verbrennen.

In den vergangenen Wochen hatte Hitler sowohl in Afrika, als auch
in Russland Erfolge zu verzeichnen. Die Folge davon war, dass der Optimismus auf der einen, die Bestürzung und der Pessimismus auf der anderen
Seite des Volkes mit einer der deutschen Trägheit unvergleichlichen
Schnelligkeit anstieg. Allenthalben hörte man unter den Gegnern Hitlers,
also unter dem besseren Teil des Volkes, Klagerufe, Worte der Enttäuschung und der Entmutigung, die nicht selten in dem Ausruf endigten:
"Sollte nun Hitler doch...?"

Indessen ist der deutsche Angriff auf Ägypten zum Stillstand
gekommen, Rommel muss in einer gefährlich exponierten Lage verharren -
aber noch geht der Vormarsch im Osten weiter. Dieser scheinbare Erfolg
ist unter den grauenhaftesten Opfern erkauft worden, sodass er schon
nicht mehr als vorteilhaft bezeichnet werden kann. Wir warnen daher vor
j e d e m Optimismus.

Wer hat die Toten gezählt, Hitler oder Goebbels - wohl keiner von
beiden. Täglich fallen in Russland Tausende. Es ist die Zeit der Ernte,
und der Schnitter fährt mit vollem Zug in die reife Saat. Die Trauer
kehrt ein in die Hütten der Heimat, und niemand ist da, der die Tränen
der Mütter trocknet. Hitler aber belügt die, deren teuerstes Gut er geraubt und in den sinnlosen Tod getrieben hat.

Jedes Wort, das aus Hitlers Munde kommt, ist Lüge: Wenn er Frieden
sagt, meint er den Krieg, und wenn er in frevelhaftester Weise den Namen
des Allmächtigen nennt, meint er die Macht des Bösen, den gefallenen
Engel, den Satan. Sein Mund ist der stinkende Rachen der Hölle und seine
Macht ist im Grunde verworfen. Wohl muss man mit rationalen Mitteln den
Kampf wider den nationalsozialistischen Terrorstaat führen; wer aber
heute noch an der realen Existenz der dämonischen Mächte zweifelt, hat
den metaphysischen Hintergrund dieses Krieges bei weitem nicht begriffen.
Hinter dem Konkreten, hinter dem sinnlich wahrnehmbaren, hinter allen
sachlichen logischen Ueberlegungen, steht das Irrationale, d.i. der Kampf
wider den Dämon, wider den Boten des Antichrists. Ueberall und zu allen
Zeiten haben die Dämonen im Dunkeln gelauert auf die Stunde, da der Mensch
schwach wird, da er seine ihm von Gott auf Freiheit gegründete Stellung
im ordo eigenmächtig verlässt, da er dem Druck des Bösen nachgibt, sich
von den Mächten höherer Ordnung loslöst und so, nachdem er den ersten
Schritt freiwillig getan, zum zweiten und dritten und immer mehr getrieben wird mit rasend steigender Geschwindigkeit - überall und zu allen
Zeiten der höchsten Not sind Menschen aufgestanden, Propheten, Heilige,
die ihre Freiheit gewahrt hatten, die auf den Einzigen Gott hinwiesen
und mit seiner Hilfe das Volk zur Umkehr mahnten. Wohl ist der Mensch
frei, aber er ist wehrlos wider das Böse ohne den wahren Gott, er ist
wie ein Schiff ohne Ruder, dem Sturme preisgegeben, wie ein Säugling
ohne Mutter, wie eine Wolke, die sich auflöst.

Gibt es, so frage ich Dich, der Du ein Christ bist, gibt es in
diesem Ringen um die Erhaltung Deiner höchsten Güter ein Zögern, ein
Spiel mit Intrigen, ein Hinausschieben der Entscheidung in der Hoffnung,
dass ein anderer die Waffen erhebt, um Dich zu verteidigen? Hat Dir nicht
Gott selbst die Kraft und den Mut gegeben zu kämpfen? Wir m ü s s e n
das Böse dort angreifen, wo es am mächtigsten ist, und es ist am mächtigsten in der Macht Hitlers.

"Ich wandte mich und sah an alles Unrecht, das geschah
unter der Sonne; und siehe, da waren Tränen derer, so Unrecht
litten und hatten keinen Tröster; und die ihnen Unrecht taten,
waren zu mächtig, dass sie keinen Tröster haben konnten.
Da lobte ich die Toten, die schon gestorben waren, mehr
denn die Lebendigen, die noch das Leben hatten....." (Sprüche)

Novalis: "Wahrhafte Anarchie ist das Zeugungselement der
Religion. Aus der Vernichtung alles Positiven hebt sie ihr glorreiches Haupt als neue Weltstifterin empor... Wenn Europa
wieder erwachen wollte, wenn ein Staat der Staaten, eine politische Wissenschaftslehre uns bevorstände! Sollte etwa die
Hierarchie.. ..das Prinzip des Staatenvereins sein?.....Es
wird solange Blut über Europa strömen, bis die Nationen ihren
fürchterlichen Wahnsinn gewahr werden, der sie im Kreis herumtreibt, und von heiliger Musik getroffen und besänftigt, zu
ehemaligen Altären in bunter Vermischung treten, Werke des
Friedens vornehmen und ein grosses Friedensfest auf den rauchenden Walstätten mit heissen Tränen gefeiert wird. Nur
die Religion kann Europa wieder aufwecken und das Völkerrecht
sichern und die Christenheit mit neuer Herrlichkeit sichtbar
auf Erden in ihr friedenstiftendes Amt installieren."

Wir weisen eindrücklich darauf hin, dass die Weisse Rose nicht im
Solde einer ausländischen Macht steht. Obgleich wir wissen, dass die
nationalsozialistische Macht militärisch gebrochen werden muss, suchen
wir eine Erneuerung des schwerverwundeten deutschen Geistes von Innen
her zu erreichen. Dieser Wiedergeburt muss aber die klare Erkenntnis
aller Schuld, die das deutsche Volk auf sich geladen hat, und ein
rücksichtsloser Kampf gegen Hitler und seine allzuvielen Helfershelfer,
Parteimitglieder, Quislinge usw., vorangehen. Mit aller Brutalität muss
die Kluft zwischen dem besseren Teil des Volkes und allem, was mit dem
Nationalsozialismus zusammenhängt, aufgerissen werden. Für Hitler und sei
ne Anhänger gibt es auf dieser Erde keine Strafe, die ihren Taten gerech
wäre. Aber aus Liebe zu kommenden Generationen muss nach Beendigung
des Krieges ein Exempel statuiert werden, daß niemand auch nur die geringste Lust je verspüren sollte, Aehnliches aufs neue zu versuchen.
Vergesst auch nicht die kleinen Schurken dieses Systems, merkt Euch
die Namen, aufdass keiner entkomme! Es soll ihnen nicht gelingen, in
letzter Minute noch nach all diesen Scheusslichkeiten die Fahne zu
wechseln und so zu tun, als ob nichts gewesen wäre!

Zu Ihrer Beruhigung möchten wir noch hinzufügen, dass die Adressen
der Leser der Weissen Rose irgendwo schriftlich niedergelegt sind.
Die Adressen sind willkürlich Adressbüchern entnommen.

Wir schweigen nicht, wir sind Euer böses Gewissen, die Weisse
Rose lässt Euch keine Ruhe!

Bitte vervielfältigen und weitersenden!

Flugblätter der Weißen Rose IV

Es ist eine alte Weisheit, die man Kindern immer wieder aufs neue predigt, dass, wer nicht hören will, fühlen muss. Ein kluges Kind wird sich aber die Finger nur einmal am heißen Ofen verbrennen.

In den vergangenen Wochen hatte Hitler sowohl in Afrika, als auch in Russland Erfolge zu verzeichnen. Die Folge davon war, dass der Optimismus auf der einen, die Bestürzung und der Pessimismus auf der anderen Seite des Volkes mit einer der deutschen Trägheit unvergleichlichen Schnelligkeit anstieg. Allenthalben hörte man unter den Gegnern Hitlers, also unter dem besseren Teil des Volkes, Klagerufe, Worte der Enttäuschung und der Entmutigung, die nicht selten in dem Ausruf endigten: 'Sollte nun Hitler doch...?'

Indessen ist der deutsche Angriff auf Ägypten zum Stillstand gekommen, Rommel muss in einer gefährlich exponierten Lage verharren aber noch geht der Vormarsch im Osten weiter. Dieser scheinbare Erfolg ist unter den grauenhaftesten Opfern erkauft worden, so dass er schon nicht mehr als vorteilhaft bezeichnet werden kann. Wir warnen daher vor j e d e m Optimismus.

Wer hat die Toten gezählt, Hitler oder Goebbels — wohl keiner von beiden. Täglich fallen in Russland Tausende. Es ist die Zeit der Ernte, und der Schnitter fährt mit vollem Zug in die reife Saat.

Pamphlets of the White Rose IV

There is an old and wise saying, which we preach to children time and again, that 'he who will not listen, must feel'.[1] However, clever children will burn their fingers on a hot stove only once.

In the past few weeks,[2] Hitler has claimed successes both in Africa and in Russia. The consequence of this is that optimism on the one hand, and dismay and pessimism on the other, have risen among the people with a speed which is wholly unlike the usual German complacency. Everywhere among the opponents of Hitler, that is, among the better part of the people, we hear lamentations, words of disappointment and discouragement, ending not infrequently with the interjection: 'What if Hitler after all…?'

Meanwhile, the German offensive against Egypt has ground to a halt — Rommel must remain in a dangerously exposed position, but the advance in the East still proceeds. This apparent success comes at the most hideous cost to human life, so much so that already it can no longer be claimed advantageous. We therefore warn against optimism IN ANY FORM.

Who has counted the dead, Hitler or Goebbels? — neither of them, in truth. Thousands fall in Russia every day. It is harvest-time, and the Reaper cuts into the ripe crop with broad strokes.

Die Trauer kehrt ein in die Hütten der Heimat und niemand
ist da, der die Tränen der Mütter trocknet, Hitler aber belügt
die, deren teuerstes Gut er geraubt und in den sinnlosen Tod
getrieben hat.

Jedes Wort, das aus Hitlers Munde kommt, ist Lüge.
Wenn er Frieden sagt, meint er den Krieg, und wenn er in
frevelhaftester Weise den Namen des Allmächtigen nennt,
meint er die Macht des Bösen, den gefallenen Engel, den Satan.
Sein Mund ist der stinkende Rachen der Hölle, und seine
Macht ist im Grunde verworfen. Wohl muss man mit
rationalen Mitteln den Kampf wider den nationalsozialistischen
Terrorstaat führen; wer aber heute noch an der realen Existenz
der dämonischen Mächte zweifelt, hat den metaphysischen
Hintergrund dieses Krieges bei weitem nicht begriffen. Hinter
dem Konkreten, hinter dem sinnlich Wahrnehmbaren, hinter
allen sachlichen, logischen Überlegungen steht das Irrationale,
d.i. der Kampf wider den Dämon, wider den Boten des
Antichrists. Überall und zu allen Zeiten haben die Dämonen
im Dunkeln gelauert auf die Stunde, da der Mensch schwach
wird, da er seine ihm von Gott auf Freiheit gegründete Stellung
im ordo eigenmächtig verlässt, da er dem Druck des Bösen
nachgibt, sich von den Mächten höherer Ordnung loslöst und
so, nachdem er den ersten Schritt freiwillig getan, zum zweiten
und dritten und immer mehr getrieben wird mit rasend
steigender Geschwindigkeit —

FLUGBLÄTTER | PAMPHLETS 165

Grief settles into the country's cottages, and no-one is there to dry the mothers' tears. Hitler, however, lies to those whose most precious possessions he has stolen and driven to a meaningless death.

Every word that comes out of Hitler's mouth is a lie. When he says 'peace', he means 'war', and when he blasphemously invokes the name of the Almighty, he means the power of the Evil One, of the fallen angel, of Satan. His mouth is the stinking maw of Hell, and his power is, in its very essence, corrupt. We must undoubtedly lead a struggle against the National Socialist terror state by rational means, but whoever today still doubts the genuine existence of demonic powers has woefully failed to grasp the metaphysical background of this war. Behind the concrete, behind that which is discernible to the senses, behind all factual, logical considerations, there lies the Irrational, i.e. the fight against the demon, against the messenger of the Antichrist. Everywhere and always, demons have lurked in the darkness, waiting for the day on which man would become weak; the day on which he would forsake his position in the divine order,[3] freely ordained for him by God; the day on which he would surrender to the forces of the Evil One, unbind himself from the powers of a higher order and, having taken the first step of his own volition, be then driven forcibly towards taking the second and third steps at an ever more furious pace.

überall und zu allen Zeiten der höchsten Not sind Menschen aufgestanden, Propheten, Heilige, die ihre Freiheit gewahrt hatten, die auf den Einzigen Gott hinwiesen und mit seiner Hilfe das Volk zur Umkehr mahnten. Wohl ist der Mensch frei, aber er ist wehrlos wider das Böse ohne den wahren Gott, er ist wie ein Schiff ohne Ruder, dem Sturme preisgegeben, wie ein Säugling ohne Mutter, wie eine Wolke, die sich auflöst.

Gibt es, so frage ich Dich, der Du ein Christ bist, gibt es in diesem Ringen um die Erhaltung Deiner höchsten Güter ein Zögern, ein Spiel mit Intrigen, ein Hinausschieben der Entscheidung in der Hoffnung, dass ein anderer die Waffen erhebt, um Dich zu verteidigen? Hat Dir nicht Gott selbst die Kraft und den Mut gegeben zu kämpfen? Wir m ü s s e n das Böse dort angreifen, wo es am mächtigsten ist, und es ist am mächtigsten in der Macht Hitlers.

'Ich wandte mich und sah an alles Unrecht, das geschah unter der Sonne; und siehe, da waren Tränen derer, so Unrecht litten und hatten keinen Tröster; und die ihnen Unrecht taten, waren so mächtig, dass sie keinen Tröster haben konnten. Da lobte ich die Toten, die schon gestorben waren, mehr denn die Lebendigen, die noch das Leben hatten....' (Sprüche)

Novalis: 'Wahrhafte Anarchie ist das Zeugungselement der Religion. Aus der Vernichtung alles Positiven hebt sie ihr glorreiches Haupt als neue Weltstifterin empor...

In all places and at all times when man has found himself most in need, men have taken a stand; prophets and saints who, in asserting their freedom[4], have pointed towards the one and only God and, with His help, beseeched the people to reverse their course.[5] Man is undoubtedly free, but he is defenceless in the face of evil without the one true God: he is like a ship[6] without a rudder, abandoned to the storm; like a nursing child without a mother; like a cloud that disperses.[7]

And so I ask you — you who proclaim yourself Christian — do you waver in this struggle for the preservation of your highest Goods?[8] Is there a calculation, deferring your decision in the hope that someone else will raise their weapons to defend you? Did not God himself endow you with the strength and courage to fight? We MUST make an assault upon evil where it is strongest, and it is strongest in the hands of Hitler.

'So I returned, and considered all the oppressions that are done under the sun; and behold the tears of such as were oppressed, and they had no comforter; and on the side of their oppressors there was power; but they had no comforter.

Therefore I praised the dead which are already dead more than the living who are yet alive....' (Ecclesiastes)[9]

Novalis: 'True anarchy is the generative element of religion. Out of the annihilation of all that is positive she raises her glorious head aloft, as the new foundress of the world...

Wenn Europa wieder erwachen wollte, wenn ein Staat der Staaten, eine politische Wissenschaftslehre bevorstände! Sollte etwa die Hierarchie... das Prinzip des Staatenvereins sein?... Es wird so lange Blut über Europa strömen, bis die Nationen ihren fürchterlichen Wahnsinn gewahr werden, der sie im Kreis herumtreibt, und von heiliger Musik getroffen und besänftigt zu ehemaligen Altären in bunter Vermischung treten, Werke des Friedens vornehmen und ein großes Friedensfest auf den rauchenden Walstätten mit heißen Tränen gefeiert wird. Nur die Religion kann Europa wieder aufwecken und das Völkerrecht sichern und die Christenheit mit neuer Herrlichkeit sichtbar auf Erden in ihr friedenstiftendes Amt installieren.'

Wir weisen ausdrücklich darauf hin, dass die Weiße Rose nicht im Solde einer ausländischen Macht steht. Obgleich wir wissen, dass die nationalsozialistische Macht militärisch gebrochen werden muss, suchen wir eine Erneuerung des schwerverwundeten deutschen Geistes von innen her zu erreichen. Dieser Wiedergeburt muss aber die klare Erkenntnis aller Schuld, die das deutsche Volk auf sich geladen hat, und ein rücksichtsloser Kampf gegen Hitler und seine allzuvielen Helfershelfer, Parteimitglieder, Quislinge usw. vorausgehen. Mit aller Brutalität muss die Kluft zwischen dem besseren Teil des Volkes und allem, was mit dem Nationalsozialismus zusammenhängt, aufgerissen werden.

Oh, if Europe were to reawaken, and a state of states, a theory of political science, were to confront us! Should hierarchy then... be the principle of the union of states? Blood will flow over Europe until the nations become aware of the frightful madness which drives them in circles; until, struck by celestial music and pacified, they approach their former altars as a colourful collective, compose works of peace and hold a great festival of peace, hot tears falling upon the smouldering battlefields. Only religion can re-awaken Europe, protect the rights of the peoples, and swear Christendom into its peace-making office, its new splendour visible on earth.'[10]

We want to make clear that the actions of the White Rose are not being done in the service of some foreign power. Although we know that National Socialism's hold on power can only be broken through military force,[11] we are attempting to reawaken the gravely wounded German spirit from within. This rebirth must, however, be preceded by full recognition of the guilt with which the German people have burdened themselves, and by a ruthless battle against Hitler and his all too numerous accomplices, party members, Quislings,[12] and so on. The gulf between the better part of society and those who choose to associate with National Socialism must be torn apart with uncompromising brutality.

Für Hitler und seine Anhänger gibt es auf dieser Erde keine Strafe, die ihren Taten gerecht wäre. Aber aus Liebe zu kommenden Generationen muss nach Beendigung des Krieges ein Exempel statuiert werden, dass niemand auch nur die geringste Lust je verspüren sollte, Ähnliches aufs neue zu versuchen. Vergesst auch nicht die kleinen Schurken dieses Systems, merkt Euch die Namen, auf dass keiner entkomme! Es soll ihnen nicht gelingen, in letzter Minute noch nach diesen Scheußlichkeiten die Fahne zu wechseln und so zu tun, als ob nichts gewesen wäre!

Zu Ihrer Beruhigung möchten wir noch hinzufügen, dass die Adressen der Leser der Weißen Rose nirgendwo schriftlich niedergelegt sind. Die Adressen sind willkürlich Adressbüchern entnommen.

Wir schweigen nicht, wir sind Euer böses Gewissen; die Weiße Rose lässt Euch keine Ruhe!

Bitte vervielfältigen und weitersenden!

There is no punishment on this earth that would do justice to the crimes of Hitler and his inner circle. But out of love for the coming generations, an example must be set after the end of the war, so that no one will ever feel even the slightest inclination to commit such acts again. Do not forget the petty villains of this regime; remember their names, so that not a single one goes free! They should not be allowed to switch sides at the last minute, after committing such abhorrent crimes, and act as though nothing had happened!

We would like to add for your reassurance that the addresses of White Rose readers are nowhere recorded in writing. The addresses are taken at random from directories.[13]

We will not be silent. We are your bad conscience. The White Rose will never leave you in peace!

Please duplicate and re-distribute!

Notes

[1] This is a similar proverb to 'once bitten, twice shy'. The leaflet takes a sarcastic tone pointing to the hypocrisy of impressing this upon children while German adults do not act in accordance with the proverb.

[2] From the end of May to the beginning of July 1942.

[3] German: 'im ordo'. The leaflet develops the Augustinian idea from the third leaflet (III, 18ff.) that God endowed man with a nature between that of an angel and a beast. According to Augustine, if man remembers this endowment and obeys the divine order, then he acquires the immortality of the angel. If, however, he abuses his free will and forgets, disobediently and with bestial desire, his endowment, then he forfeits himself to death and hell (*De civitate Dei*, Book 12, Chapter 21).

[4] 'Freiheit': 'freedom'. See the glossary.

[5] Here there is a stark theological implication related to the Greek notion of Metanoia: change in one's way of life resulting from penitence or spiritual conversion. See Matthew 18:2-5: 'He called a little child to him, and placed the child among them. And he said: "Truly I tell you, unless you change and become like little children, you will never enter the kingdom of heaven. Therefore, whoever takes the lowly position of this child is the greatest in the kingdom of heaven. And whoever welcomes one such child in my name welcomes me.'

[6] This is a recurrent theological-didactic equation. See the second recitative in Johann Sebastian Bach's solo cantata 'Ich

will den Kreuzstab gerne tragen' (BWV 56) from his third cycle in which life is likened to a sea voyage with death as the ultimate destination.

[7] A reference to the Wisdom of Solomon 2:4: 'our life will be undone like the trace of a cloud and will be dispersed like mist, pursued by the rays of the sun and oppressed by its heat.'

[8] 'Deiner höchsten Güter': 'your highest goods'. These are the Goods endowed by God as part of man's place in divine order: the knowledge of good and evil, man's duty to God's creation, man's responsibility for his own actions, righteousness and peace.

[9] This refers to Ecclesiastes 4:1-2 in which the following arguments are put forward: oppression and evil deeds are vanity; the strength of two is better than one; and better is a poor and wise child than an old and foolish king. See also Ecclesiastes 4:3: 'yea, better than both of them is he who hath not yet been, who hath not seen the evil work that is done under the sun.' This is picked up in Luke 23:29: 'Look, the days are coming when people will say, "Blessed are the barren women, the wombs that never bore, and breasts that never nursed".' See also Johannes Brahms' *Ich wandte mich und sahe an* (op. 121 no. 2 (1896)).

[10] Novalis (Friedrich von Hardenberg), *Die Christenheit oder Europa* (1799), written in the light of the French Revolution, which Novalis perceived as chaotic and irreligious. Within his speech, Novalis explores the possibility of a new Europe based on poetical Christendom (these particularly poetic excerpts

were taken from around six pages of the original text) and inspired by Friedrich Schleiermacher's *Über die Religion* (1799). [11] By 1942, it was too late to consider any solution other than to defeat National Socialism by military means.

[12] 'Quisling': a term referring to a person who collaborates with the enemy (traitor), originating from the surname of Vidkun Quisling, who headed a Nazi collaborationist regime (the National Union) in Norway under the supervision of Nazi administrator, Josef Terboven, during World War Two. The term was first used by Norwegian Labour Party politician Oscar Torp in a 1933 newspaper interview to describe Quisling's followers; eventually a puppet government was established with Quisling as Prime Minister between 1942 and 1945.

[13] The discovery of the addresses of communists in 1933 and 1934 led to the brutal destruction of their party.

Translated by Adam Mazarelo, Emily Rowland, and Amy Wilkinson.

THE FIFTH PAMPHLET

January 1943

6.

Flugblätter der Widerstandsbewegung in Deutschland.

Aufruf an alle Deutsche !

Der Krieg geht seinem sicheren Ende entgegen. Wie im Jahre
1918 versucht die deutsche Regierung alle Aufmerksamkeit auf
die wachsende U-Bootgefahr zu lenken, während im Osten die Armeen
unaufhörlich zurückeströmen, im Westen die Invasion erwartet wird.
Die Rüstung Amerikas hat ihren Höhepunkt noch nicht erreicht,
aber heute schon übertrifft sie alles in der Geschichte seither
Dagewesene. Mit mathematischer Sicherheit führt Hitler das deutsche
Volk in den Abgrund. H i t l e r   k a n n   d e n   K r i e g   n i c h t
g e w i n n e n ,   n u r   n o c h   v e r l ä n g e r n ! Seine
und seiner Helfer Schuld hat jedes Mass unendlich überschritten.
Die gerechte Strafe rückt näher und näher !

Was aber tut das deutsche Volk? Es sieht nicht, und es hört
nicht. Blindlings folgt es seinen Irrführern ins Verderben. Sieg
um jeden Preis, haben sie auf ihre Fahne geschrieben. Ich kämpfe
bis zum letzten Mann , sagt Hitler - indes ist der Krieg bereits
verloren.

Deutsche! Wollt Ihr und Eure Kinder dasselbe Schicksal erleiden,
das den Juden widerfahren ist? Wollt Ihr mit dem gleichen Masse
gemessen werden, wie Eure Verführer? Sollen wir auf ewig das von
aller Welt gehasste und ausgestossene Volk sein? Nein! Darum
trennt Euch von dem nationalsozialistischen Untermenschentum!
Beweist durch die Tat, dass Ihr anders denkt! Ein neuer Befreiungskrieg bricht an. Der bessere Teil des Volkes kämpft auf unserer
Seite. Zerreisst den Mantel der Gleichgültigkeit, den Ihr um Euer
Herz gelegt! Entscheidet Euch, e h '   e s   z u   s p ä t   i s t !

Glaubt nicht der nationalsozialistischen Propaganda, die
Euch den Bolschewistenschreck in die Glieder gejagt hat! Glaubt
nicht, dass Deutschlands Heil mit dem Sieg des Nationalsozialismus
auf Gedeih und Verderben verbunden sei! Ein Verbrechertum kann
keinen deutschen Sieg erringen. Trennt Euch r e c h t z e i t i g
von allem, was mit dem Nationalsozialismus zusammenhängt! Nachher
wird ein schreckliches, aber gerechtes Gericht kommen über die,
so sich feig und unentschlossen verborgen hielten.

Was lehrt uns der Ausgang dieses Krieges, der nie ein nationaler war?

Der imperialistische Machtgedanke muss, von welcher Seite er
auch kommen möge, für alle Zeit unschädlich gemacht werden. Ein
einseitiger preussischer Militarismus darf nie mehr zur Macht
gelangen. Nur in grosszügiger Zusammenarbeit der europäischen
Völker kann der Boden geschaffen werden, auf welchem ein neuer
Aufbau möglich sein wird. Jede zentralistische Gewalt, wie sie
der preussische Staat in Deutschland und Europa auszuüben versucht
hat, muss im Keime erstickt werden. Das kommende Deutschland
kann nur föderalistisch sein. Nur eine gesunde föderalistische
Staatenordnung vermag heute noch das geschwächte Europa mit
neuem Leben zu erfüllen. Die Arbeiterschaft muss durch einen
vernünftigen Sozialismus aus ihrem Zustand niedrigster Sklaverei
befreit werden. Das Truggebilde der autarken Wirtschaft muss in
Europa verschwinden. Jedes Volk, jeder Einzelne hat ein Recht
auf die Güter der Welt!

Freiheit der Rede, Freiheit des Bekenntnisses, Schutz des
einzelnen Bürgers vor der Willkür verbrecherischer Gewaltstaaten,
das sind die Grundlagen des neuen Europa.

Unterstützt die Widerstandsbewegung, verbreitet die Flugblätter!

Flugblätter der Widerstandsbewegung in Deutschland.

A u f r u f a n a l l e D e u t s c h e !

Der Krieg geht seinem sicheren Ende entgegen. Wie im Jahre 1918 versucht die deutsche Regierung alle Aufmerksamkeit auf die wachsende U-Boot-Gefahr zu lenken, während im Osten die Armeen unaufhörlich zurückströmen, im Westen die Invasion erwartet wird. Die Rüstung Amerikas hat ihren Höhepunkt noch nicht erreicht, aber heute schon übertrifft sie alles in der Geschichte seither Dagewesene. Mit mathematischer Sicherheit führt Hitler das deutsche Volk in den Abgrund. H i t l e r k a n n d e n K r i e g n i c h t g e w i n n e n , n u r n o c h v e r l ä n g e r n ! Seine und seiner Helfer Schuld hat jedes Maß unendlich überschritten. Die gerechte Strafe rückt näher und näher!

Was aber tut das deutsche Volk? Es sieht nicht und es hört nicht. Blindlings folgt es seinen Verführern ins Verderben. Sieg um jeden Preis! haben sie auf ihre Fahne geschrieben. Ich kämpfe bis zum letzten Mann, sagt Hitler — indes ist der Krieg bereits verloren.

Deutsche! Wollt Ihr und Eure Kinder dasselbe Schicksal erleiden, das den Juden widerfahren ist? Wollt Ihr mit dem gleichen Maße gemessen werden wie Eure Verführer? Sollen wir auf ewig das von aller Welt gehasste und ausgestoßene Volk sein? Nein!

Pamphlets of the Resistance Movement in Germany.

AN APPEAL TO ALL GERMANS!

The war is heading towards its certain end. Just as in 1918, the German government is trying to channel all attention towards the growing threat of submarines, while in the East the armies are constantly falling back, and in the West the invasion is expected. America's armament has not yet reached its full potential, but even now it exceeds anything ever seen before in history. With mathematical certainty, Hitler is leading the German people into the abyss. HITLER CANNOT WIN THE WAR; HE CAN ONLY PROLONG IT! His guilt and the guilt of his followers continually exceeds all boundaries. Just punishment is nigh!

But what are the Germans doing about it? They refuse to see, and they refuse to hear. Blindly they follow their corrupters into ruin.[1] 'Victory at all costs!', they wrote on their banner. I will fight until the last man, Hitler says — meanwhile, the war is already lost.

Germans! Do you and your children want to suffer the same fate that befell the Jews? Do you want to be judged by the same measures as those who have corrupted you? Shall we be forever hated and shunned by the whole world? No!

Darum trennt Euch von dem nationalsozialistischen Untermenschentum! Beweist durch die Tat, dass Ihr anders denkt! Ein neuer Befreiungskrieg bricht an. Der bessere Teil des Volkes kämpft auf unserer Seite. Zerreißt den Mantel der Gleichgültigkeit, den Ihr um Euer Herz gelegt! Entscheidet Euch, e h ' e s z u s p ä t i s t!

Glaubt nicht der nationalsozialistischen Propaganda, die Euch den Bolschewistenschreck in die Glieder gejagt hat! Glaubt nicht, dass Deutschlands Heil mit dem Sieg des Nationalsozialismus auf Gedeih und Verderben verbunden sei! Ein Verbrechertum kann keinen deutschen Sieg erringen. Trennt Euch r e c h t z e i t i g von allem, was mit dem Nationalsozialismus zusammenhängt! Nachher wird ein schreckliches, aber gerechtes Gericht kommen über die, so sich feig und unentschlossen verborgen hielten.

Was lehrt uns der Ausgang dieses Krieges, der nie ein nationaler war?

Der imperialistische Machtgedanke muss, von welcher Seite er auch kommen möge, für alle Zeit unschädlich gemacht werden. Ein einseitiger preußischer Militarismus darf nie mehr zur Macht gelangen. Nur in großzügiger Zusammenarbeit der europäischen Völker kann der Boden geschaffen werden, auf welchem ein neuer Aufbau möglich sein wird.

So separate yourselves from the subhuman nature of National Socialism![2] Act — prove that you think differently! A new fight for liberation is at hand. The better part of the people is fighting on our side. Tear off the cloak of indifference that shrouds your heart! Decide — BEFORE IT'S TOO LATE!

Don't believe the National Socialist propaganda that has injected the fear of Bolshevism into your every limb! Don't believe that Germany's salvation is bound to the victory of National Socialism for better or worse! A band of criminals cannot bring about German victory. Break away from everything associated with National Socialism BEFORE IT'S TOO LATE! A terrible, but a righteous judgement is coming to those who holed themselves up in such a cowardly and passive way.

What does the outcome of this war teach us, a war in which it was never our nation that was at stake?

The imperial concept of power, regardless of which side it might come from, needs to be neutralised for all time. A one-sided Prussian militarism should never be allowed to come to power again. Only through the generous collaboration of the European nations can the foundation be built on which a new development will be possible.

Jede zentralistische Gewalt, wie sie der preußische Staat in Deutschland und Europa auszuüben versucht hat, muss im Keime erstickt werden. Das kommende Deutschland kann nur föderalistisch sein. Nur eine gesunde föderalistische Staatenordnung vermag heute noch das geschwächte Europa mit neuem Leben zu erfüllen. Die Arbeiterschaft muss durch einen vernünftigen Sozialismus aus ihrem Zustand niedrigster Sklaverei befreit werden. Das Truggebilde der autarken Wirtschaft muss in Europa verschwinden. Jedes Volk, jeder einzelne hat ein Recht auf die Güter der Welt!

Freiheit der Rede, Freiheit des Bekenntnisses, Schutz des einzelnen Bürgers vor der Willkür verbrecherischer Gewaltstaaten, das sind die Grundlagen des neuen Europa.

Unterstützt die Widerstandsbewegung, verbreitet die Flugblätter!

Every centralising force, like the one the Prussian state has tried to exercise in Germany and in Europe, must be nipped in the bud. The Germany to come can only be federalist. Only a healthy federalism can bring new life to a weakened Europe. The workers need to be freed from their condition of abject slavery through a level-headed socialism. This delusion of a self-sufficient economy must disappear from Europe. Every nation, every person has a right to the goods of the world!

Freedom of speech, freedom of faith, protection of the individual citizen from the despotism of criminal and violent states: these are the foundations of the new Europe.

Support the resistance movement, <u>distribute</u> the pamphlets!

Notes

[1] 'Verführer': 'corrupter', 'seducer'. The German word echoes the word 'Führer', the title used by Adolf Hitler.

[2] 'Untermenschentum': 'sub-humanity'. See the glossary.

Translated by Ilona Clayton and Ro Crawford.

THE SIXTH PAMPHLET

February 1943

5

Kommilitoninnen! Kommilitonen!

Erschüttert steht unser Volk vor dem Untergang der Männer von Stalingrad. Dreihundertdreissigtausend deutsche Männer hat die geniale Strategie des Weltkriegsgefreiten sinn- und verantwortungslos in Tod und Verderben gehetzt. Führer, wir danken dir!

Es gärt im deutschen Volk: Wollen wir weiter einem Dilettanten das Schicksal unserer Armeen anvertrauen? Wollen wir den niedrigen Machtinstinkten einer Parteiclique den Rest der deutschen Jugend opfern? Nimmermehr! Der Tag der Abrechnung ist gekommen, der Abrechnung unserer deutschen Jugend mit der verabscheuungswürdigsten Tyrannis, die unser Volk je erduldet hat. Im Namen der ganzen deutschen Jugend fordern wir von dem Staat Adolf Hitlers die persönliche Freiheit, das kostbarste Gut des Deutschen zurück, um das er uns in der erbärmlichsten Weise betrogen hat.

In einem Staat rücksichtsloser Knebelung jeder freien Meinungsäusserung sind wir aufgewachsen. HJ, SA, SS haben uns in den fruchtbarsten Bildungsjahren unseres Lebens zu uniformieren, zu revolutionieren, zu narkotisieren versucht. "Weltanschauliche Schulung" hiess die verächtliche Methode, das keimende Selbstdenken und Selbstwerten in einem Nebel leerer Phrasen zu ersticken. Eine Führerauslese, wie sie teuflischer und borniertes zugleich nicht gedacht werden kann, zieht ihre künftigen Parteibonzen auf Ordensburgen zu gottlosen, schamlosen und gewissenlosen Ausbeutern und Mordbuben heran, zur blinden, stupiden Führergefolgschaft. Wir "Arbeiter des Geistes" wären gerade recht, dieser neuen Herrenschicht den Knüppel zu machen. Frontkämpfer werden von Studentenführern und Gauleiteraspiranten wie Schuljungen gemassregelt, Gauleiter greifen mit geilen Spässen den Studentinnen an die Ehre. Deutsche Studentinnen haben an der Münchner Hochschule auf die Besudelung ihrer Ehre eine würdige Antwort gegeben, deutsche Studenten haben sich für ihre Kameradinnen eingesetzt und standgehalten. Das ist ein Anfang zur Erkämpfung unserer freien Selbstbestimmung, ohne die geistige Werte nicht geschaffen werden können. Unser Dank gilt den tapferen Kameradinnen und Kameraden, die mit leuchtendem Beispiel vorangegangen sind!

Es gibt für uns nur eine Parole: Kampf gegen die Partei! Heraus aus den Parteigliederungen, in denen man uns politisch weiter mundtot halten will! Heraus aus den Hörsälen der SS- Unter- oder Oberführer und Parteikriecher! Es geht uns um wahre Wissenschaft und echte Geistesfreiheit! Kein Drohmittel kann uns schrecken, auch nicht die Schliessung unserer Hochschulen. Es gilt den Kampf jedes einzelnen von uns um unsere Zukunft, unsere Freiheit und Ehre in einem seiner sittlichen Verantwortung bewussten Staatswesen.

Freiheit und Ehre! Zehn lange Jahre haben Hitler und seine Genossen die beiden herrlichen deutsche Worte bis zum Ekel ausgequetscht, abgedroschen, verdreht, wie es nur Dilettanten vermögen, die die höchsten Werte einer Nation vor die Säue werfen. Was ihnen Freiheit und Ehre gilt, haben sie in zehn Jahren der Zerstörung aller materiellen und geistigen Freiheit, aller sittlichen Subatanz im deutschen Volk genugsam gezeigt. Auch dem dümmsten Deutschen hat das furchtbare Blutbad die Augen geöffnet, das sie im Namen von Freiheit und Ehre der deutschen Nation in ganz Europa angerichtet haben und täglich neu anrichten. Der deutsche Name bleibt für immer geschändet, wenn nicht die deutsche Jugend endlich aufsteht, rächt und sühnt zugleich, seine Peiniger zerschmettert und ein neues, geistiges Europa aufrichtet.

Studentinnen! Studenten! Auf uns sieht das sieht das deutsche Volk! Von uns erwartet es, wie 1813 die Brechung des Napoleonischen, so 1943 die Brechung des nationalsozialistischen Terrors aus der Macht des Geistes. Beresina und Stalingrad flammen im Osten auf, die Toten von Stalingrad beschwören uns!

"Frisch auf, mein Volk, die Flammenzeichen rauchen!"

Unser Volk steht im Aufbruch gegen die Verknechtung Europas durch den Nationalsozialismus, im neuen gläubigen Durchbruch von Freiheit und Ehre!

Kommilitoninnen! Kommilitonen!

Erschüttert steht unser Volk vor dem Untergang der Männer von Stalingrad. Dreihundertdreißigtausend deutsche Männer hat die geniale Strategie des Weltkriegsgefreiten sinn- und verantwortungslos in Tod und Verderben gehetzt. Führer, wir danken dir!

Es gärt im deutschen Volk: Wollen wir weiter einem Dilettanten das Schicksal unserer Armeen anvertrauen? Wollen wir den niedrigsten Machtinstinkten einer Parteiclique den Rest unserer deutschen Jugend opfern? Nimmermehr!

Der Tag der Abrechnung ist gekommen, der Abrechnung der deutschen Jugend mit der verabscheuungswürdigsten Tyrannis, die unser Volk je erduldet hat. Im Namen der ganzen deutschen Jugend fordern wir vom Staat Adolf Hitlers die persönliche Freiheit, das kostbarste Gut der Deutschen zurück, um das er uns in der erbärmlichsten Weise betrogen hat.

In einem Staat rücksichtsloser Knebelung jeder freien Meinungsäußerung sind wir aufgewachsen. HJ, SA und SS haben uns in den fruchtbarsten Bildungsjahren unseres Lebens zu uniformieren, zu revolutionieren, zu narkotisieren versucht. 'Weltanschauliche Schulung' hieß die verächtliche Methode, das aufkeimende Selbstdenken und Selbstwerten in einem Nebel leerer Phrasen zu ersticken.

Fellow students!

Our people look on the defeat of our men at Stalingrad with revulsion. The ingenious strategy of our Great War corporal[1] has hounded three hundred thousand German men senselessly and irresponsibly to death and ruin. Führer, we thank you![2]

Turmoil is fermenting among the German people: are we to further entrust the fate of our armies to a dilettante? Are we to sacrifice what is left of our German youth to the basest power-grabbing instincts of a party clique? No more!

The day of reckoning has come, the reckoning of Germany's youth with the most heinous tyranny that our people has ever endured. In the name of all German youth we demand from Adolf Hitler's state the return of our personal freedom, that treasure which Germans hold most dear, and which he has taken from us in the most wretched of ways.

We have grown up in a state which ruthlessly gags all freedom of expression. The Hitler Youth, the SA, and the SS have tried to homogenise, radicalise and anaesthetise us in the most fruitful of our formative years. 'Ideological Education' is the term they use for their contemptible method of suffocating burgeoning independent thought and self-esteem with a fog of empty rhetoric.

Eine Führerauslese, wie sie teuflischer und zugleich bornierter nicht gedacht werden kann, zieht ihre künftigen Parteibonzen auf Ordensburgen zu gottlosen, schamlosen und gewissenlosen Ausbeutern und Mordbuben heran, zur blinden, stupiden Führergefolgschaft. Wir 'Arbeiter des Geistes' wären gerade recht, dieser neuen Herrenschicht den Knüppel zu machen. Frontkämpfer werden von Studentenführern und Gauleiteraspiranten wie Schulbuben gemaßregelt, Gauleiter greifen mit geilen Späßen den Studentinnen an die Ehre. Deutsche Studentinnen haben an der Münchner Hochschule auf die Besudelung ihrer Ehre eine würdige Antwort gegeben, deutsche Studenten haben sich für ihre Kameradinnen eingesetzt und standgehalten. Das ist ein Anfang zur Erkämpfung unserer freien Selbstbestimmung, ohne die geistige Werte nicht geschaffen werden können. Unser Dank gilt den tapferen Kameradinnen und Kameraden, die mit leuchtendem Beispiel vorangegangen sind!

Es gibt für uns nur eine Parole: Kampf gegen die Partei! Heraus aus den Parteigliederungen, in denen man uns politisch weiter mundtot halten will! Heraus aus den Hörsälen der SS-Unter- und -Oberführer und Parteikriecher! Es geht uns um wahre Wissenschaft und echte Geistesfreiheit! Kein Drohmittel kann uns schrecken, auch nicht die Schließung unserer Hochschulen. Es gilt den Kampf jedes einzelnen von uns um unsere Zukunft, unsere Freiheit und Ehre in einem seiner sittlichen Verantwortung bewussten Staatswesen.

The Nazi elite, who could not be any more diabolical or narrow-minded, groom their future party bigwigs in the *Ordensburgen*[3] to become godless, shameless, unscrupulous, exploitative, murderous scoundrels, the blind and brainless entourage of the Führer. We, 'Workers of the Mind',[4] would be fully justified in smashing this new ruling class. Student leaders and aspiring Gauleiters[5] reprimand front-line soldiers like schoolboys, Gauleiters insult the honour of our female students with lewd jokes. Women studying at Munich University have given a dignified response to the assault on their honour, and their male counterparts have come out in support of them and are standing firm. This is a first step in the fight for our free self-determination, without which spiritual values cannot be forged. We are grateful to the brave students who are lighting the way!

For us there is only one slogan: fight against the party! Get out of the party structures which stifle our political expression! Get out of the lecture halls of the SS and senior leaders and party sycophants! Our goal is true scholarship and real freedom of the mind! There is no threat that can deter us, not even the closure of our universities. It is the duty of each and every one of us to fight for our future, our freedom and honour in a political system conscious of its own moral responsibility.

Freiheit und Ehre! Zehn lange Jahre haben Hitler und seine Genossen die beiden herrlichen deutschen Worte bis zum Ekel ausgequetscht, abgedroschen, verdreht, wie es nur Dilettanten vermögen, die die höchsten Werte einer Nation vor die Säue werfen. Was ihnen Freiheit und Ehre gilt, das haben sie in zehn Jahren der Zerstörung aller materiellen und geistigen Freiheit, aller sittlichen Substanz im deutschen Volk genugsam gezeigt. Auch dem dümmsten Deutschen hat das furchtbare Blutbad die Augen geöffnet, das sie im Namen von Freiheit und Ehre der deutschen Nation in ganz Europa angerichtet haben und täglich neu anrichten. Der deutsche Name bleibt für immer geschändet, wenn nicht die deutsche Jugend endlich aufsteht, rächt und sühnt zugleich, ihre Peiniger zerschmettert und ein neues geistiges Europa aufrichtet.

Studentinnen! Studenten! Auf uns sieht das deutsche Volk! Von uns erwartet es, wie 1813 die Brechung des Napoleonischen, so 1943 die Brechung des nationalsozialistischen Terrors aus der Macht des Geistes.

Beresina und Stalingrad flammen im Osten auf, die Toten von Stalingrad beschwören uns!

'Frisch auf mein Volk, die Flammenzeichen rauchen!'

Unser Volk steht im Aufbruch gegen die Verknechtung Europas durch den Nationalsozialismus, im neuen gläubigen Durchbruch von Freiheit und Ehre!

Freedom and honour! For ten long years, Hitler and his cronies have trivialised, distorted, and bled dry these two glorious German words to the point of disgust, as only dilettantes know how, casting a nation's highest ideals before swine. They have shown well enough what freedom and honour mean to them during the ten years in which they have destroyed all material and spiritual freedom, all moral substance of the German people. Even the most dull-witted German has had his eyes opened by the terrible bloodbath, which, in the name of the freedom and honour of the German nation, they have unleashed upon Europe, and unleash anew each day. The German name will remain forever tarnished unless finally the German youth stands up, pursues both revenge and atonement, smites our tormentors, and founds a new intellectual Europe.

Students! The German people look to us! The responsibility is ours: just as the power of the spirit broke the Napoleonic terror in 1813, so too will it break the terror of the National Socialists in 1943.

To the east, Berezina[6] and Stalingrad have gone up in flames, the dead of Stalingrad beseech us!

'Rise up, my people, the beacons are aflame!'[7]

Our people are on the verge of breaking free from National Socialism's enslavement of Europe in this new spiritual dawn of freedom and honour!

Notes

[1] This is a mocking reference to Adolf Hitler, who had been a corporal during the First World War.

[2] 'Führer, wir danken dir': a slogan used at Nazi rallies and in propaganda. Here it is used sarcastically.

[3] 'Ordensburgen': training schools for the future Nazi elite.

[4] Arbeiter des Geistes': a reference to a term used in Nazi propaganda to refer to intellectuals/students.

[5] 'Gauleiter': an official in charge of a district in the Third Reich.

[6] After the retreat of Napoleon's Grande Armée following their defeat in Moscow in October 1914 where they suffered many losses, they crossed over the Berezina river.

[7] This quotation is taken from the patriotic poem 'Soldatenlied' ('Soldier's Song'), written by the poet and soldier Theodor Körner during the German Campaign of 1813.

Translated by Sophie Bailey and Finn Provan.

EXHIBITION CATALOGUE

Alexandra Lloyd

This is an edited version of the catalogue which accompanied the exhibition 'The White Rose: Reading, Writing, Resistance', held at the Taylor Institution Library in October and November 2018. There is, of course, a good deal more to be said about the White Rose group than can be presented in a handful of exhibition cabinets. Our intention was to show a snapshot of their lives, their resistance activities, and their enduring legacy, through examples of what they read and wrote. The exhibition displayed items from the world-class holdings of the Taylor Institution Library and the Bodleian Library. Where possible we have exhibited editions comparable or identical to those which the White Rose members read. We also included information and artefacts relating to the Nazi book burnings, older examples of resistance through reading and writing, and the White Rose's legacy in literature and film.

THE WHITE ROSE
Reading · Writing · Resistance

Exhibition: Voltaire Room, Taylor Institution, St Giles', OX13NA, open to Bodleian card holders from 12-31 October 2018. Opening times: Mon-Fri 9am-6.30pm | Sat 10am-3pm.

Exhibition Launch: 12 October 2018, 5pm, Room 2, Taylor Institution. RSVP to alexandra.lloyd@seh.ox.ac.uk.

www.whiteroseproject.org

Figure 5. Poster advertising the exhibition 'The White Rose: Reading, Writing, Resistance' held at the Taylor Institution, October–November 2018.

Cabinet 1 — The White Rose Resistance Group

Sibylle Bassler, *Die Weiße Rose: Zeitzeugen erinnern sich* (Reinbek: Rowohlt, 2006)

The White Rose Group extended beyond Munich, and many individuals were involved. Sibylle Bassler's 2006 text *Die Weiße Rose: Zeitzeugen erinnern sich* (*The White Rose: Witnesses Remember*) brings together accounts by many of those who knew the Scholls and had assisted in, been aware of, or participated in the group's activities, including Elisabeth Hartnagel, Traute Lafrenz, Anneliese Knoop-Graf, Jürgen Wittenstein, Lilo Fürst-Ramdohr, Franz J. Müller, Susanne Zeller-Hirzel, and Hildegard Hamm-Brücher.

Kurt Huber, *Leibniz* (Munich: Oldenbourg, 1951)

Kurt Huber taught philosophy and music at the Ludwig Maximilian University in Munich. His lectures were popular with students, including members of the White Rose. During his sentencing on 19 April 1943, Huber was referred to as 'a blemish against German scholarship' ('ein Schandfleck der deutschen Wissenschaft').[1] The presiding judge declared: 'The days when every man can be allowed to profess his own political "beliefs" are past. For us there is but one standard: the National Socialist one. Against this we measure each man!'[2]

---

[1] Cited in Klaus Drobisch, *Wir schweigen nicht: Eine Dokumentation über den antifaschistischen Kampf Münchner Studenten 1942/43* (Berlin: Union-Verlag VOB, 1968), p. 134.

[2] Cited in Inge Scholl, The *White Rose: Munich 1942–1943*, trans. by Arthur R. Schultz (Middletown, CT: Wesleyan University Press, 1983), p. 127. 'Die Zeiten, wo jeder mit einem eigenen politischen "Glauben"

Huber was working on a biography of the philosopher Leibniz when he was arrested and continued to do so throughout his imprisonment. He was executed on 13 July 1943. Huber's manuscript was published posthumously by his wife and his research assistant. After Huber's death, the government billed his wife for the costs of the execution.

Two students, Hans Leipelt (1921-1945) and Marie-Luise Jahn (1918-2010), made copies of the sixth White Rose pamphlet and distributed them in Hamburg. They also collected money for Huber's widow, and it was while doing this that they were caught, tried, and sentenced. Jahn received a 12-year prison sentence. Leipelt was sentenced to death and executed at Stadelheim Prison on 29 January 1945.

Inge Scholl, *Die Weiße Rose* (Frankfurt A.M.: Fischer, 1956)

One of the most important accounts of the White Rose was written by one of the Scholl siblings, Inge, and first published in West Germany in 1952. *Die Weiße Rose* (*The White Rose*) is a document of witness, consisting of a first-person retrospective account by Inge Scholl, as well as copies of the leaflets, documents from the first two White Rose trials, and eye-witness statements. It has been published in several editions since the 1950s.

---

herumlaufen konnte, sind vorbei! Für uns gibt es nur noch *ein* Maß, das nationalsozialistische. Danach messen wir alle!', cited in Drobisch, *Wir schweigen nicht*, p. 134.

Cabinet 2 — How reading shaped the path to resistance

We know that Hans and Sophie had been enthusiastic members of the Hitler Youth, so what made their attitudes shift? One answer may lie in the fact that they were voracious readers. Their letters and diaries make frequent mention of the books they and their friends were reading, and they sometimes read communally, reading passages aloud in turn. By looking at what they read, we also get a valuable insight into the character of these young people. The materials here show some examples of the literature that influenced their intellectual and moral development.

Georges Bernanos, *Journal d'un curé de campagne* (*The Diary of a Country Priest*) (Paris: Plon, 1936)

In the winter of 1940 Sophie went on a skiing trip in Tyrol with some of her siblings and friends. In the evenings they read aloud from Georges Bernanos' novel, *Journal d'un curé de campagne* (*The Diary of a Country Priest*). Set in Ambricourt (northern France), it tells the story of a new priest struggling with the responsibilities of his parish. Bernanos was a fierce critic of Hitler and German fascism. *The Diary of a Country Priest* obviously made a great impression on Sophie who recommended the work to her fiancé Fritz Hartnagel.

Gottfried Keller, 'Die öffentlichen Verleumder', in *Sämtliche Werke*, ed. by Jonas Fränkel & Carl Helbling (Bern; Leipzig: Benteli, 1926–1949), pp. 338–39

On 1 May 1942 Sophie arrived in Munich to begin her studies. Eight days later she celebrated her 21st birthday with a party, together with Hans, Christoph Probst, Alexander Schmorell, and others. In the course of the festivities the friends played a game: they each had to recite a poem and the others should guess who it was by. Hans came up with a poem which no-one knew, and no-one could guess the author. It turned out to be Gottfried Keller's 'Die öffentlichen Verleumder' ('The Public Slanderers'), a poem written in response to the public vilification of a Zurich hospital director in 1878. There were obvious parallels with their own political situation, and the friends jokingly suggested that they should duplicate and distribute the poem. The Munich students' party ended in the Englischer Garten — a large park near the university — where they drank and sang while Hans played the guitar and Alexander played the balalaika.

Fyodor Dostoevsky, Двойник (Harmondsworth: Penguin, 1970)

On a skiing trip taken by Sophie, Hans, and others in the winter of 1941, they took turns reading aloud from Fyodor Dostoevsky's novella *The Double* (1846), in which a government clerk (possibly) encounters his *doppelgänger*. This was part of a much more profound engagement with Russian literature and culture which would affect Hans deeply. On 23 July 1942, Hans, Willi Graf, and Alexander Schmorell set off for a three-month tour of duty at the Russian front. During this period Hans came firmly to reject Nazi assertions that the Russians were inferior, writing in his diary in August 1942:

> We Germans don't have Dostoyevsky or Gogol. Nor Pushkin nor Turgenev. What about Goethe and Schiller? someone retorts. Who does? A scholar. When did you last read Goethe? I don't recall — in school or somewhere. I ask a Russian: What writers do you have? Oh, says the

Russian, we have them all, all of them. [...] What Russian is this? A peasant, a washerwoman, a mailman.[3]

Thomas Mann, *Der Zauberberg* (Berlin: Fischer, 1925)

Before she was permitted to begin her undergraduate studies, Sophie Scholl had to complete six months of Reichsarbeitsdienst (National Labour Service) at a labour camp 45 miles from Ulm. During this time, she read Augustine's *Confessions*, and Thomas Mann's *Der Zauberberg* (*The Magic Mountain*, 1924), having read and enjoyed *Buddenbrooks* (1901). She was not supposed to have any books but received special permission from her supervisor. She found it difficult to fit in with the other girls and used her books as a way of distancing herself from them (she commented rather disparagingly on some of the girls who kept with them a copy of Goethe's *Faust* to look erudite!).

Thomas Mann, *Deutsche Hörer: 55 Radiosendungen nach Deutschland* (Göttingen: Wallstein, 1945)

Thomas Mann was in exile in America during the war. He contributed regularly to the BBC German Service and on 27 June

---

[3] Hans Scholl, diary entry, 22 August 1942, in *At the Heart of the White Rose: Letters and Diaries of Hans and Sophie Scholl*, ed. by Inge Jens, trans. by J. Maxwell Brownjohn (Walden, NY: Plough Publishing House, 2017), pp. 254–55. 'Wir Deutschen haben weder Dostojewsky noch Gogol. Weder Puschkin noch Turgenjew. Aber Goethe, Schiller, antwortet jemand. Wer sagt dies? Ein Gebildeter. Wann hast du zuletzt Goethe gelesen? Ich weiß es nicht mehr, auf der Schule oder ich weiß nicht wo. Ich frage einen Russen. Welchen Dichter habt ihr? O, antwortet dieser, alle, alle haben wir [...]. Wer ist dieser Russe? Ein Bauer, eine Waschfrau, ein Briefträger', Hans Scholl and Sophie Scholl, *Briefe und Aufzeichnungen*, ed. by Inge Jens (Frankfurt a.M.: Fischer Taschenbuch Verlag, 1988), p. 123.

1943 Mann dedicated his broadcast to the White Rose. His addresses were published in German as *Deutsche Hörer: 55 Radiosendungen nach Deutschland von Thomas Mann* (*German Listeners: 55 Radio Messages to Germany by Thomas Mann*).

Theodor Haecker, *Schöpfer und Schöpfung* (Leipzig: J. Hegner, 1934)

An important influence on the group was the writer and translator Theodor Haecker, an authority on Kierkegaard and translator of works by John Henry Cardinal Newman. Under the Nazis, Haecker was banned from speaking publicly or publishing. On 4 February 1943 Haecker met with a group of around thirty-five people; among them were members of the White Rose group. Haecker read from his unpublished journal, and from his 1934 work *Schöpfer und Schöpfung* (*Creator and Creation*), in which he discusses man's place in a fallen world.

Theodor Haecker, *Tag- und Nachtbücher* (Innsbruck: Haymon, 1989)

Following the execution of Hans and Sophie Scholl and Christoph Probst in February 1943, Haecker's apartment was searched by the Gestapo. He realised during the search that the manuscript of his journal — which would become his *Tag- und Nachtbücher* (published in English as *Journal in the Night* in 1950) — was lying on the coffee table. This journal, in which he documented his internal resistance against the Nazis, is an important work of inner exile writing. It was only thanks to the quick thinking and bravery of his teenaged daughter that the manuscript was not discovered. She deftly put it in her music bag and, when questioned by the Gestapo agents, told them it contained simply sheet music for her piano lesson. They let her leave without examining the bag's contents and she got the manuscript to safety.

Cabinet 3 — Banned books and book burnings

'Dort, wo man Bücher verbrennt, verbrennt man am Ende auch Menschen'
(Heinrich Heine, 1821).

Under the Nazis, a list of banned authors was compiled and published by the Reichsministerium für Volksaufklärung und Propaganda (Reich Ministry of Public Enlightenment and Propaganda). Authors, living and dead, were banned for being of Jewish descent, or because of their political convictions. Those suspected of Communist or pacifist sympathies were also banned.

Erich Maria Remarque, *Im Westen nichts Neues* (Berlin: Propyläen Verlag, 1929)

On 10 May 1933 tens of thousands of people gathered in the pouring rain at Opernplatz in Berlin as books were burned. The event was part of a campaign organised by the German Student Union who called on students and citizens to 'cleanse' their libraries and throw anything 'un-German' onto the fire. Erich Maria Remarque's anti-war novel *Im Westen nichts Neues* (*All Quiet on the Western Front*) was one of those to be burned. In his speech at the event, the Propaganda Minister Josef Goebbels declared: 'Against literary betrayal of the soldiers of the World War, for educating the people in the spirit of truth! I commit to the flames the writings of Erich Maria Remarque.'[4]

Judith Kerr, *When Hitler stole Pink Rabbit* (London: Collins, 1971)

Among the many authors publically condemned by Goebbels at the book burning in May 1933 was the journalist Alfred Kerr. His daughter, Judith Kerr, would go on to write about their escape from Germany in her internationally acclaimed autobiographical novel, *When Hitler Stole Pink Rabbit* (1971).

Franz Kafka, *Metamorphosis* (Leipzig: Wolff, 1917)

In 1933 works by Jewish authors were banned. Only Schocken Books was permitted to publish works by Jewish writers, on the condition that they only be sold to Jews. Schocken had been given the publication rights to Franz Kafka's collected works in 1931, and in 1935 they published his unfinished novel, *Der Prozess* (*The Trial*). When Kafka's works were banned, Schocken moved some of its production to Prague, and in 1939 the publishing house rellocated to Palestine where Kafka's works were first published in Hebrew. Schocken also set up a publishing house in New York where the philosopher and Holocaust survivor Hannah Arendt worked as an editor. Writing in 1944, Arendt commented: 'The reader of Kafka's stories is very likely to pass through a stage during which he will be

---

[4] Cited in Léon Poliakov, *Das Dritte Reich und seine Denker* (Grunewald: Arani-Verlags-GmbH, 1978), p. 121 (my translation). 'Gegen literarischen Verrat am Soldaten des Weltkrieges, für Erziehung des Volkes im Geist der Wahrhaftigkeit! Ich übergebe dem Feuer die Schriften des Erich Maria Remarque.'

inclined to think of Kafka's nightmare world as a trivial though, perhaps, psychologically interesting forecast of a world to come. But this world actually has come to pass.'[5]

Stefan Zweig, *Sternstunden der Menschheit: Fünf historische Miniaturen* (Leipzig: Insel, 1927)

Inge Scholl recounts an episode from Hans's days in the Hitler Youth. He was reading a volume by his then favourite author, Stefan Zweig, an Austrian Jew who left Austria following Hitler's rise to power. Hans's Hitler Youth leader saw what Hans was reading — a collection of historical miniatures about events that changed history — and reacted as follows: 'One of the leaders snatched out of his hands a book by his favourite author, *Sternstunden der Menschheit* by Stefan Zweig. It was banned, he was told. But why? There was no answer.'[6] The content of the text was unimportant. Only the identity of its author mattered.

Heinrich Heine, *Buch der Lieder* (Longmans: Green & co, 1920)

A story is told about Sophie and one of her favourite writers, Heinrich Heine. In 1936, when Sophie was active in the Hitler

---

[5] Hannah Arendt, 'Franz Kafka: A Revaluation', in *Essays in Understanding, 1930–1954*, ed. by Jerome Kohn (New York: Harcourt Brace & Company, 1994), p. 73.

[6] Scholl, *The White Rose: Munich 1942–1943*, p. 8. 'Einer der Führer hatte ihm das Buch seines Lieblingsdichters aus der Hand genommen, Stefan Zweigs 'Sternstunden der Menschheit'. Das sei verboten, hatte man ihm gesagt. Warum? Darauf gab es keine Antwort', Scholl, *Die Weiße Rose* (Frankfurt a.M.: Verlag der Frankfurter Hefte, 1982), p. 18.

Youth, an important leader of the Bund deutscher Mädel (League of German Girls) visited the local group in Ulm where the Scholls lived. At this meeting, Sophie reportedly suggested that they read and discuss poems by Heine. The leader, obviously appalled at the idea, declared that Heine was a Jewish writer whose works had been banned and burned. Sophie replied: 'Anyone who doesn't know Heine, doesn't know German literature' ('Wer Heinrich Heine nicht kennt, kennt die deutsche Literatur nicht').[7]

Ernst Wiechert, *Der Dichter und die Zeit: Rede, gehalten am 16. April 1935 im Auditorium Maximum der Universität München* (Zurich: Artemis, 1945)

Ernst Wiechert was a teacher and writer strongly opposed to Nazism. A speech he gave to students at the Ludwig Maximilian University in April 1935, in which he criticised Nazi policies, was smuggled out of Germany in a loaf of bread so that it could be published abroad. The Scholls had a copy. When in 1938 Wiechert spoke out against the internment of the theologian and pastor Martin Niemöller, he himself was sent to Buchenwald concentration camp for three months.

Erich Kästner, *Emil und die Detektive* (Zurich: Atrium, 1958)

Erich Kästner's books were among those burned on the Opernplatz on 10 May 1933, and Kästner in fact was there to see it happen. His 1929 novel for children, *Emil und die Detektive* (*Emil and the Detectives*), was the only one of his works to escape the flames, as it was deemed sufficiently apolitical and popular to be spared, though

---

[7] Cited in Ernest M. Wolf, *Blick auf Deutschland: Kleine Skizzen zur deutschen Kulturkunde* (New York: Scribner, 1966), p. 113 (my translation).

in 1936 the decision was taken to ban it. Despite being viewed by the Nazis as an 'undesirable author' ('unerwünschter Autor'), he was permitted to write screenplays, and under two pseudonyms worked on films for UFA (Universum Film AG), the principal film company in the Third Reich. Many have subsequently criticised Kästner's decision to remain in the Third Reich.

Cabinet 4 — Writing and Resistance in the German Context

The White Rose used the written word to call the German people to resist Nazism and to contribute to an end to the Second World War. They distributed pamphlets — *Flugblätter* — to spread their ideas and to reach as many individuals as possible. The 'Flugblatt' was the first medium of mass communication, and in the history of the German-speaking lands we find pamphlets and flyers used to disseminate ideas and information, for the purposes of propaganda and control, as well as provocation and resistance. Initially flyers were sold rather than distributed free of charge. It is estimated that in the 1520s a four-page pamphlet would have cost a 'pfennig' ('penny') — the equivalent of a mug of beer.

Martin Luther, *An den christlichen Adel deutscher Nation* (Augsburg: Hans von Erfurt, 1520) and *Von der Freyheit eines Christenmenschen* (Vuittenbergae: Melchior Lotter the Younger, 1521)

The development of the printing press and movable type meant that texts could be reproduced rapidly and in significant numbers. Indeed, without the printing press, Martin Luther's ideas would not have spread as quickly as they did. The first of Luther's three Reformation treatises, *An den christlichen Adel deutscher Nation* (*To the Christian Nobility of the German Nation*), appeared in August 1520. Here, he mounted an attack on what he viewed as the 'three walls of the Romanists', three points of Church and Papal authority with which he disagreed. This pamphlet was followed by *Von der Freyheit eines Christenmenschen* (*A Treatise on Christian Liberty*) in November 1520 in which Luther further explored the idea of justification by faith.

Georg Büchner, *Der Hessische Landbote* (Gütersloh: S. Mohn, 1965)

In 1834 the writer Georg Büchner was involved in a secret society dedicated to revolution and overthrowing the ruling powers. He produced an eight-page political text in collaboration with Friedrich Ludwig Weidig, a school teacher and theologian, and around 1200 copies were distributed. The pamphlet, *Der Hessische Landbote* (*The Hessian Messenger*) was highly controversial: using emotive and Biblical language, it exposed the corruption of the authorities in the Grand Duchy of Hessen-Darmstadt and called on the rural population to revolt. The main text was preceded by instructions on what to do with the pamphlet, including that it should be kept hidden from police. It begins with a slogan coined in 1792 and borrowed from the French Revolution: 'Peace to the peasants! War on the palaces!' ('Friede den Hütten! Krieg den Palästen!').[8] Two of Büchner's co-conspirators were arrested and Büchner, for whose arrest a warrant was issued, managed to flee across the French border to Strasbourg. Weidig was later arrested and died in 1837 in mysterious circumstances while incarcerated.

---

[8] Georg Büchner, *Der Hessische Landbote*, ed. by Uwe Jansen (Stuttgart: Reclam, 2016), p. 5 (my translation).

Cabinet 5 — The White Rose Pamphlets

Johann Wolfgang von Goethe, *Des Epimenides Erwachen* (Berlin: Duncker und Humboldt, 1817)

The first pamphlet quoted from works by Johann Wolfgang von Goethe and Friedrich Schiller, both of whom had been co-opted by the Nazis for their nationalist cause. Goethe's play *Des Epimenides Erwachen* (*Epimenides Awakes*) was written for the celebrations in Berlin of Napoleon's defeat in 1815. It is significant that the final word of the excerpt quoted in the leaflet is 'Freiheit!' ('freedom'). When Sophie was taken to the court from her cell on the morning of 22 February 1943, her cell mate noted that she had left behind the court's indictment on which she had written a single word: 'Freiheit!'. Sophie was executed that same day at 5pm. Minutes later, it was her brother's turn. As he was led to the guillotine Hans cried out 'Es lebe die Freiheit!' ('Long live freedom!').

Friedrich Schiller, 'Die Gesetzgebung des Lykurgus und Solon', *Schillers Sämtliche Werke*, ed. by Richard Fester (Stuttgart: Cotta, 1904-1905), vol. 13: Historische Schriften I, pp. 67–105

The first leaflet quotes from Schiller's 1789 essay 'Die Gesetzgebung des Lykurgus und Solon' (*The Lawgiving of Lycurgus and Solon*), in which he contrasts the oligarchic and republican forms of government. Sophie had been at university for about six weeks, when she caught sight of a leaflet calling for resistance. This was the first of the White Rose's pamphlets. By chance, when waiting for Hans in his room not long after, she happened to flick through his books, and found a passage of Schiller's text that had been marked. It was the same passage that had struck her in the White Rose pamphlet.

She is reported to have confronted her brother and at this point became involved in the White Rose activities.[9]

Cabinet 6 — The White Rose's Legacy in Literature and Film

The legacy of the White Rose can be found all over Germany today. Many places have streets, squares, and schools named after the Scholl siblings. You can even see a waxwork of Sophie Scholl at the Madame Tussauds in Berlin. In 2003, a series broadcast on the German television channel ZDF had a competition to find the nation's favourite German: *Our Best — The Greatest Germans* (*Unsere Besten — Die größten Deutschen*). In the final vote, Konrad Adenauer (first chancellor of West Germany, 1949–1963) achieved the top spot, followed by Martin Luther and Karl Marx, and then in fourth position by Hans and Sophie Scholl. Sophie was the only woman to make the top ten which also included Bach, Goethe, and Bismarck.

Michael Verhoeven, *Die Weiße Rose* (Kinowelt Home Entertainment, 2006)

In 1982 two film adaptations of the history of the White Rose appeared in West Germany: Percy Adlon's *Fünf letzte Tage* (*Five Last Days*) which was broadcast on West German television, and Michael Verhoeven's feature film *Die Weiße Rose* (*The White Rose*) which was an unmitigated box office hit. The same actress, Lena Stolze, plays Sophie Scholl in both productions. Verhoeven's film was significant in exposing a bizarre legal situation: a closing title declared that the sentences against the White Rose were still considered legal by the Federal Court: the Nazi court's decisions had

---

[9] Scholl, *The White Rose*, pp. 32–34.

never been formally rescinded. There was a public outcry and in 1985 the German Parliament passed a resolution negating the verdicts.

Marc Rothemund, *Sophie Scholl — Die letzten Tage* (Drakes Avenue Pictures, 2005)

Marc Rothemund's 2005 film *Sophie Scholl — Die letzten Tage* (*Sophie Scholl — The Final Days*) is a painstakingly researched and deeply moving portrayal of Sophie and the White Rose group. The film received multiple awards and was nominated for an Oscar for Best Foreign Language Film.

Heiner Lünstedt und Ingrid Sabisch, *Sophie Scholl: Die Comic-Biografie* (Munich: Knesebeck, 2015)

Comics and graphic novels provide a singular way to explore and portray historical events and narratives. This 2015 graphic novel, *Sophie Scholl: The Comic-Biography* presents Sophie's life and legacy, from her first encounter with Fritz Hartnagel (to whom she would later become engaged), to the mass distribution of the sixth leaflet by the Allies in July 1943.

Rolf Hochhuth, *Eine Liebe in Deutschland* (Reinbek bei Hamburg: Rowohlt, 1978)

Christa Wolf, *Störfall: Nachrichten eines Tages* (Darmstadt: Luchterhand, 1987)

One of Germany's leading literary awards, the Geschwister-Scholl-Preis (Scholl Siblings Prize), is awarded annually by the State Association of Bavaria. Its first recipient was Rolf Hochhuth in 1980 for his novel *Eine Liebe in Deutschland* (*A Love in Germany*). The plot centres on a German woman who falls in love with a Polish prisoner of war in the early 1940s, for which he is executed, and she is sent to a concentration camp. In 1987 Christa Wolf received the prize for her text *Störfall: Nachrichten eines Tages* (*Accident: A Day's News*) in which the narrator reflects on the 1986 Chernobyl disaster, when one of four reactors at the nuclear power station overheated and exploded.

Die weiße Rose: Der Widerstand von Studenten gegen Hitler, München 1942/43 (Munich: Weiße Rose Stiftung, 1994)

The Weiße Rose Stiftung (White Rose Foundation) in Munich works to 'uphold the memory and legacy of the resistance group'. It was founded in 1987 by members and relatives of the White Rose and other supporters. They have a permanent exhibition at the Ludwig-Maximilians-Universität in Munich, the DenkStätte Weiße Rose, and offer a range of events including educational workshops and a travelling exhibition. This publication, *The White Rose: Students' Resistance Against Hitler, Munich 1942/1943*, outlines the foundation's activities.

Further Reading on the White Rose

Sibylle Bassler, *Die Weiße Rose: Zeitzeugen erinnern sich* (Reinbek: Rowohlt, 2006)

Ulrich Chaussy and Gerd R. Ueberschär, *'Es lebe die Freiheit!' Die Geschichte der Weißen Rose und ihrer Mitglieder in Dokumenten und Berichten* (Frankfurt a.M.: Fischer Taschenbuch, 2013)

Klaus Drobisch, *Wir schweigen nicht: Eine Dokumentation über den antifaschistischen Kampf Münchner Studenten 1942/43* (Berlin: Union-Verlag VOB, 1968)

Annette Dumbach and Jud Newborn, *Sophie Scholl and the White Rose* (Oxford: Oneworld Publications, 2007)

Miriam Gebhardt, *Die Weiße Rose: Wie aus ganz normalen Deutschen Widerstandskämpfer wurden* (Munich: Deutsche Verlags-Anstalt, 2017)

Willi Graf, *Briefe und Aufzeichnungen*, ed. by Anneliese Knoop-Graf and Inge Jens (Frankfurt a.M.: Fischer, 1994)

Richard Hanser, *A Noble Treason: The Revolt of the Munich Students against Hitler* (San Francisco, CA: Ignatius Press, 2012)

Thomas Hartnagel (ed.), *Damit wir uns nicht verlieren: Briefwechsel 1937-1943* (Frankfurt a.M.: Fischer, 2006)

Wolfgang Huber (ed.), *Die Weiße Rose: Kurt Hubers letzte Tage* (Munich: Utz Verlag, 2018)

Inge Jens (ed.), *At the Heart of the White Rose: Letters and Diaries of Hans and Sophie Scholl*, trans. by J. Maxwell Brownjohn (Walden, NY: Plough Publishing House, 2017)

—., *Hans Scholl, Sophie Scholl: Briefe und Aufzeichnungen* (Frankfurt a.M.: Fischer Taschenbuch Verlag, 1988)

Jakob Knab, *Ich schweige nicht: Hans Scholl und die Weiße Rose* (Darmstadt: wbg Theiss, 2018)

Heiner Lünstedt und Ingrid Sabisch, *Sophie Scholl: Die Comic-Biografie* (Munich: Knesebeck, 2015)

Frank McDonough, *Sophie Scholl: The Real Story of the Woman Who Defied Hitler* (Stroud: The History Press, 2010)

Alexander Schmorell and Christoph Probst, *Gesammelte Briefe*, ed. by Christiane Moll (Berlin: Lukas Verlag, 2011)

Inge Scholl, *Die Weiße Rose* (Frankfurt a.M.: Verlag der Frankfurter Hefte, 1952)

—., *The White Rose: Munich, 1942-1943* (Middletown: Wesleyan University Press USA, 1983),

Paul Shrimpton, *Conscience before Conformity: Hans and Sophie Scholl and the White Rose Resistance in Nazi Germany* (Leominster: Gracewing, 2017)

Hinrich Siefken (ed.), *Die Weiße Rose und ihre Flugblätter: Dokumente, Texte, Lebensbilder, Erläuterungen* (Manchester: University of Manchester Press, 1993)

—., *Die Weiße Rose: Student Resistance to National Socialism, 1942–1943: Forschungsergebnisse und Erfahrungsberichte: A Nottingham Symposium* (Nottingham: University of Nottingham, 1991)

Ethel Tolansky, *Sophie Scholl and the White Rose: Resistance to the Nazis*, trans. by Helena Scott (London: Catholic Truth Society, 2012)

CPSIA information can be obtained
at www.ICGtesting.com
Printed in the USA
LVHW050200290122
709548LV00008B/313

9 780995 456440